The entrepreneurial personality

ROUTLEDGE SMALL BUSINESS SERIES
Edited by David Storey

Helping Small Firms Grow: An implementation approach
Christopher J. Hull and Benny Hjern

Barriers to Growth in Small Firms
J. S. Barber, S. Metcalfe and M. Porteous

The Performance of Small Firms
David Storey, Kevin Keasey, Robert Watson and Pooran Wynarczyck

Small and Medium-Size Enterprises and Regional Development
Edited by Maria Giaoutzi, Peter Nijkamp and David Storey

The entrepreneurial personality
Concepts, cases and categories

Elizabeth Chell
Jean Haworth
Sally Brearley

London and New York

First published 1991 by Routledge
11 New Fetter Lane, London EC4P 4EE

Simultaneously published in the USA and Canada
by Routledge
a division of Routledge, Chapman and Hall, Inc.
29 West 35th Street, New York, NY 10001

Typeset by Columns Design & Production Services Ltd, Reading
Printed and bound in Great Britain by
Biddles Ltd, Guildford and King's Lynn

British Library Cataloguing in Publication Data
Chell, Elizabeth
    The entrepreneurial personality : concepts, cases and categories. – (Small
    business series)
    1. Entrepreneurship
    I. Title   II. Series
    338.04
    ISBN 0–415–03872–3

Library of Congress Cataloging-in-Publication Data
Chell, Elizabeth.
    The entrepreneurial personality : concepts, cases, and categories /
    Elizabeth Chell, Jean M. Haworth, Sally A. Brearley.
        p.   cm. – (Routledge small business series)
    Includes bibliographical references and index.
    ISBN 0–415–03872–3
    1. Entrepreneurship – Case studies.   2. Small business – Case studies.
I. Haworth, Jean M.   II. Brearley, Sally A., 1952– .   III. Title.   IV. Series.
HB615.C62 1991   90–24136
658.4′21′019–dc20   CIP

When Herschel discovered Uranus, the German naturalist Sachs remarked sceptically: 'What guarantee have we that the planet found by him really *is* Uranus?' Equally inspired was this philosophical reflection of an Englishman: 'English is the most logical language: a knife, for instance, is called by the French *couteau*, by the Germans *messer*, and so on, whereas the English call it "a knife" which is after all what a knife really is.' (Koestler, 1964, p. 614)

Contents

List of Figures   ix
List of Tables   x
Acknowledgements   xi

1 Prologue   1
Problems and issues   1
Plan of this book   9

2 The economists' view of the entrepreneur   12
An historical perspective   13
Contemporary influences   23
Hébert and Link's taxonomy of entrepreneurial theories   26
Concluding statement   27

3 The search for entrepreneurial traits   29
The relevance of personality theory   29
*Critique of the trait approach as applied to the
   entrepreneur*   36
*The identification of profiles of entrepreneurial
   characteristics*   44
Summary and discussion   49

4 The entrepreneur in context   54
The entrepreneur as a deviant or marginal person   55
Typologies   56
The management style approach   58
The stages model   61
Contingency approaches   64
Summary   67

5 Categorisation processes and procedures   69
    Conceptual framework   69
    Method of obtaining empirical data   74
    Artificial neural networks   77
    Summary   82
    Appendix   83

6 Case studies of five business owners and their firms   86
    Eileen Bilton of Eileen Bilton Partnership Ltd   87
    Phil Boulton of LIP International   92
    Mike Murray of Cupid plc   99
    Henri Strzelecki of Henri-Lloyd Ltd   107
    Don Whitehead of VSW Scientific Instruments Ltd   115
    Discussion and conclusions   121

7 Other findings and the application of neural networks   125
    Categorisation   125
    Categorisation using neural networks   136
    Example: categorisation using network 7   138
    Discussion   143

8 Epilogue   147
    Refinements to the methodology   147
    The entrepreneurial personality   152
    Concluding statement   154

    Bibliography   156
    Author index   164
    Subject index   167

Figures

4.1 Entrepreneurial management style 59
4.2 Organisational structure and management style as they impact upon type of firm 60
5.1 Analogy between a neuron (A) and a processing element (B) 78
5.2 A multi-layer network 79
5.3 A logistic activation function 81

Tables

3.1 Perceptions of characteristics and role demands of
    entrepreneurial types and managers   50
5.1 Attributes used for the categorisation of business
    owners and their firms   76
7.1 Categorisation of thirty-one business owners and
    their firms   126
7.2 A definition of the nodes used in a three-layer
    back-propagation network   137
7.3 Comparison of network properties and prediction
    results for various sizes of hidden layer   138
7.4 Weight and bias matrices for Network 7   139
7.5 The input pattern for respondent 30 in original
    and scaled form   140
7.6 A comparison between the network and target output
    vectors for the testing set   144

Acknowledgements

We would like to thank those senior colleagues who comprised the University of Salford Research Committee 1989 for their support in making available research monies to enable this research to be carried out. We are also grateful to the Economic and Social Research Council (Grant No. F00232398) and the Nuffield Foundation (Grant No. SOC/181(1749)) for research grants which have enabled us to accumulate a body of knowledge to develop research techniques and to deepen our understanding of entrepreneurship and the entrepreneurial process, all of which has born fruit in the current project.

We owe a great debt to many business owners, located within a fifty-mile radius of the University of Salford, England. In particular we would like to thank Eileen Bilton of the Eileen Bilton Partnership Ltd, Phil Boulton of LIP International, Mike Murray of Cupid plc, Henri Strzelecki of Henri-Lloyd Ltd and Don Whitehead of VSW Scientific Instruments Ltd. We extend these thanks to twenty-six other anonymous business owners who also gave of their time freely and cheerfully and made our work so pleasurable.

Support of a different kind has come from other quarters: David Storey has been kind, generous and, in particular, patient. We are appreciative. Patience has also been an outstanding characteristic of the editorial team at Routledge: in particular, we would like to thank Rosemary Nixon and Francesca Weaver for this. Nor do we take for granted the unbegrudging and ever cheerful secretarial assistance we received from Irene Walsh whom we involved at all stages of the project. We are also grateful to Myra Fye for producing the diagrams in chapter 5.

Finally, we would like to thank our families and friends who have been so understanding during this, at times, trying period of relative neglect.

We also gratefully acknowledge permission from Richard D. Irwin Inc. to reproduce the following copyright material: Table, Perceptions of characteristics and role demands of entrepreneurial types and managers, from Timmons, J.A., Smollen, L.E. and Dingee, A.L.M. (1977), *New Venture Creation*, 1st edn, p.56; also an adapted version of the figure in Stevenson, H.H., Roberts, M.J. and Grousbeck, H.I. (1989), *New Business Ventures and the Entrepreneur*, 3rd edn, pp.18–19.

1 Prologue

In the politico-economic climate that has prevailed throughout the 1980s and continues into the 1990s, it is difficult to justify research which is basic, exploratory work with no immediately obvious practical spin-off. No apology is being made here for such an apparent indulgence. The work which is presented in the ensuing pages is primarily an attempt to address various conceptual issues concerning the entrepreneurial personality. According to some commentators, entrepreneurial research has led to a sterile debate on the characteristics of entrepreneurs with no apparent progress being made. The aims we have set ourselves are motivated, in part, by the challenge to break out of this mould. Our purpose is confined to presenting a methodology rather than a set of results to test hypotheses. Ultimately, it is intended to demonstrate a method which may be used to differentiate the entrepreneur from other business owners, and to relate types of business owner, stage of development of the business and growth orientation.

PROBLEMS AND ISSUES

Defining the entrepreneur – What are the problems?

The problem of identification of an entrepreneur has been confounded by the fact that there is still no standard, universally accepted definition of entrepreneurship. Indeed, comments such as the following only add to one's bemusement:

I would suggest that successful entrepreneurship is an art form as much as, or perhaps more than, it is an economic activity, and as such is as difficult as any other artistic activity to explain in terms of origin, method or environmental influence.

(Livesay, 1982, p.13)

It could be concluded that to persist in asking the question 'What is entrepreneurship and who are the entrepreneurs?' is likely to be a futile pursuit.

Kilby (1971) has likened the search for the entrepreneur to hunting the Heffalump. The Heffalump is a character from A.A. Milne's famous children's book *Winnie-the-Pooh* and in Kilby's words,

> [The Heffalump] is a rather large and very important animal. He has been hunted by many individuals using various ingenious trapping devices, but no one so far has succeeded in capturing him. All who claim to have caught sight of him report that he is enormous, but they disagree on his particularities. Not having explored his current habitat with sufficient care, some hunters have used as bait their own favourite dishes and have then tried to persuade people that what they caught was a Heffalump. However, very few are convinced, and the search goes on.

(Kilby, 1971, p.1)

As the entrepreneur is an elusive animal it may be better to follow the advice of Harwood (1982, p.92) who suggests, 'Know them instead by the environmental variables that mould their behaviour and determine their range!' In a survey of historic economic thought regarding entrepreneurs, Cochran (1969, p.90) writes:

> Students of entrepreneurship generally have come to agree that while it is a definable function, entrepreneur is a term denoting an ideal type rather than a term continuously applicable to a real person. Any businessman or other official may exercise entrepreneurship, but a classification cannot be devised that would empirically separate entrepreneurs from non-entrepreneurs.

Certainly the sentiment that anyone can exercise entrepreneurship is gleaning support from current thinking and research. For example, considerable work has been done to investigate the notion of the 'product champion', the innovator within an organisational context and the intrapreneur (Schon, 1965; Rothwell, 1975; Rothwell and Zegveld, 1982; Lessem, 1986a and b). Furthermore, Schultz (1975, 1980) argues that entrepreneurship need not only be applied to businessmen but could be extended to include non-market activities.

The idea that one cannot devise a classification which would separate, empirically, entrepreneurs from non-entrepreneurs has not gone unchallenged (Hoy and Carland, 1983; Timmons *et al.*, 1985). However, there is still room for debate as to how one might go about this task. For example, one approach taken assumed that entrepreneurship is a latent variable which manifests itself in various observable behaviours. By observing these behaviours and other characteristics of individuals, it was shown to be possible to assign individuals probabilistically to different categories of this latent variable (Haworth, 1988).

Reviews of the literature reveal a wide diversity of definitions of entrepreneurs and entrepreneurship and methodological approaches (Chell and Haworth, 1987; Ginsberg and Buchholtz, 1989). Definitions have included the condition that the entrepreneur be a founder, that they be owners of the firm, and/or that they may be distinguished from non-entrepreneurs by the possession of one or more behavioural characteristics. Several examples may be cited. For instance, Hull *et al.* (1980, p.11) extend the definition given in the 1972 edition of *Webster's New World Dictionary*. This definition states that the entrepreneur is:

a person who organizes and manages a business undertaking, assuming the risk for the sake of profit. . .

This they extend to include:

individuals who purchase or inherit an existing business with the intention of (and effort toward) expanding it.

This expanded definition includes many of the elements conventionally associated with lay conceptions of the entrepreneur, stressing the ideas of business expansion, risk-taking, and the profit motive. It does not, however, include the condition that an entrepreneur must necessarily be a founder.

Harwood's definition is perhaps the closest to this. He suggests that an entrepreneur is one who:

takes initiative, assumes considerable autonomy in the organisation and management of resources, shares in the asset risk, shares in an uncertain monetary profit, and innovates in more than a marginal way.

(Harwood, 1982, p.98)

Stevenson (1983), on the other hand, considers entrepreneurship to be a situational phenomenon, the essence of which is the problem of matching individuals, opportunities and required resources.

A further question arises which is: Are entrepreneurially led firms likely to be the best performers? This in itself raises some interesting questions, not the least of which is how to assess 'performance'. There is also the danger of so describing the phenomenon that the success of the business becomes a defining characteristic of the entrepreneur. For example, it has been suggested that:

> Entrepreneurs are people who have the ability to see and evaluate business opportunities; to gather the necessary resources to take advantage of them; and to initiate appropriate action to ensure success.
>
> (Meredith *et al.*, 1982, p.3)

This definition implies that the entrepreneur is assured of success. However, the authors go on to say that failure must be accepted as a learning experience and that some entrepreneurs succeed only after experiencing many failures.

The issue of business failure, especially in the early years, complicates further the problem of identification of entrepreneurs. In the United States, business failure tends to be perceived differently from the way it is perceived in the United Kingdom where there tends to be the stigma and negative connotations of having failed. Regarding business failure as a learning experience rather than a costly mistake means that successful entrepreneurs may be thought of as people who are able to acquire the necessary attributes. That is, they may possess or develop the appropriate skills and abilities for the particular business venture they have pursued, aided and abetted by an opportunity to exploit their business idea at a time when the market and other conditions are right (Timmons *et al.*, 1985). Such a general definition suggests the contingent nature of the characteristics of the entrepreneur and the fundamental importance of environmental factors. On the other hand, screening for skills such as these, as Casson (1982) has pointed out, may present considerable difficulties in practice.

The work of Carland and others has been to differentiate systematically between the entrepreneur, on the one hand, and the small business owner-manager, on the other (Hoy and Carland, 1983; Carland *et al.* 1984). In the more recent paper, Carland *et al.*

(1984, p.358) distinguish between the entrepreneur and the entrepreneurial venture, the small business owner and the small business venture:

> An entrepreneur is an individual who establishes and manages a business for the principal purposes of profit and growth. The entrepreneur is characterized principally by innovative behaviour and will employ strategic management practices in the business.
>
> An entrepreneurial venture is one that engages in at least one of Schumpeter's four categories of behaviour: that is, the principal goals of an entrepreneurial venture are profitability and growth and the business is characterized by innovative strategic practices.

In contrast to these:

> A small business owner is an individual who establishes and manages a business for the principal purpose of furthering personal goals. The business must be a primary source of income and will consume the majority of one's time and resources. The owner perceives the business as an extension of his or her personality, intricately bound with family needs and desires.
>
> A small business venture is any business that is independently owned and operated, not dominant in its field, and does not engage in any new marketing or innovative practices.

Thus, Carland *et al.* suggest that the critical defining characteristics of entrepreneurs are innovative behaviour and the ability to think and operate strategically in pursuit of their goals of business profitability and growth. Small business owners, in comparison, are concerned with securing an income through the business which will meet their immediate needs and those of their family. Small business owners are not innovators, nor are they interested in growth of the business *per se*. Many of the characteristics of this type of small business owner are well understood (Bechhofer and Elliott, 1976, 1981; Chell and Haworth, 1986; Norris, 1984).

On the other hand, these definitions of Carland and his colleagues are full of pitfalls. First it is assumed that both entrepreneurs and small business owners are founders. Second, the idea which these authors put forward for distinguishing between the motives of the entrepreneur and small business owner does not bear close scrutiny. The implication is that entrepreneurs, in developing their businesses, are not primarily pursuing their personal goals, whereas small business owners are. Third, it is unclear where the small business owner stands with regard to the profitability of the business. Fourth, the assertions that the business be a 'prime source of income' and 'consume the majority of one's time and resources' for the small business owner and not for the entrepreneur need justification. Indeed, the same comment may be applied to the idea that 'the owner perceives the business to be an extension of their personality'. Conversely, only the entrepreneur apparently can engage in 'strategic management practices'.

Ginsberg and Buchholtz (1989) observe that some definitions emphasise *autonomy* and others the *innovative* behaviour of the entrepreneur. This enables a distinction to be made between independent entrepreneurs and owner-managers. The former are highly innovative individuals who own and manage, and may have founded, an enterprise. The latter category own and manage a business, and may have founded it, but they are neither creative nor innovative as individuals. Finally, they suggest that where the condition of ownership is removed, this enables a further distinction to be made between the corporate entrepreneur who is innovative, and the corporate manager who is not.

It is clear from the above discussion that the absence of an agreed and universally accepted definition combined with conceptual obfuscation has impeded entrepreneurship research. In essence, the key problems of defining the entrepreneur exist at two levels. At the first level a problem arises from the everyday use of the term. It is often used loosely to encapsulate all business owners. On the other hand, it may be used quite narrowly to refer to a subset of business owners and, at this level, the problem is identifying the distinguishing features. Only by so doing is it clear that it is possible to distinguish the entrepreneur from the owner-manager. In the research reported in this monograph it is assumed that entrepreneurs can be distinguished from other business owners and that those key characteristics can be identified.

Categorisation

The idea of developing a typology of business owners is attractive and is often a necessary first step in exploratory research (cf. Smith, 1967; Scase and Goffee, 1980, 1982; Goffee and Scase, 1985). The problem arises when attempting to understand the categorisation process. Object categories have been described as being hierarchically ordered, comprising superordinate, basic and subordinate level categories (Rosch, 1978). This principle has been extended to the categorisation of persons (Cantor and Mischel, 1979), though not without creating somewhat obscure labels. Category membership may not be clear-cut, indeed, the boundaries between categorising concepts have been described as 'fuzzy' (Zadeh *et al.*, 1975). A potential problem, therefore, is the wrongful inclusion or exclusion of members from particular social categories.

A crucial issue with research of this nature is to be able to identify a set of characteristics which are both necessary and sufficient for category membership. The definitions discussed in the previous section suggest the following characteristics: decision autonomy and independence, creativity and innovation, risk-taking, ability to recognise and exploit opportunities, to initiate action and to pursue strategic management practices. Researchers in the field of entrepreneurship have pursued two distinct lines of inquiry: (1) to attempt to differentiate entrepreneurs from managers; (2) to differentiate entrepreneurs from other kinds of business owner. Many research studies have followed the first approach. This has clear implications for the inclusion or non-inclusion of particular characteristics. For example, it is not unreasonable to assume that decision autonomy and independence are characteristic of all business owners and therefore they will not distinguish between different types. Strategic management practice is, on the face of it, just as likely to be true of a manager as it is of an entrepreneur, though it might help to distinguish between the successful and the failing business owner.

A further issue is how, having decided upon the key defining characteristics for category membership, to identify the behavioural acts which are typical of the characteristic. For example, what acts constitute awareness and exploitation of opportunities? Could such behavioural acts have been construed as something else at the time? Is it possible to nominate a set of acts which (a) are sufficiently comprehensive, and (b) consonant with the cognitive structure of a variety of business owners such that they will be able to associate their own behaviour with those acts? Is there perhaps an alternative approach which enables the business owner to describe their behaviour in context so that the categorisation of behavioural acts is a separate exercise undertaken by the researcher at a later stage?

The starting point of this research is to suggest the following defining characteristics of entrepreneurs which distinguish them from owner-managers. At this stage they are listed and no formal definition is presented. It is part of the research process that the application of these characteristics to the entrepreneur be tested. It is therefore posited that entrepreneurs are:

- Opportunistic
- Innovative
- Creative
- Imaginative
- Ideas-people
- Proactive
- Agents of change

The notion that an entrepreneur is an agent of change has arisen from our own observations in the field. Entrepreneurs (as distinct from owner-managers) appear to thrive on change; they enjoy a lot of activity going on around them and, we would suggest, are restless and get bored easily.

The identification of behaviours which count as evidence for the attribution of such personality characteristics to the entrepreneur is clearly a crucial stage in this research process.

Neural networks

The process of categorisation of objects appears to require the systematic application of a principle, yet the categorisation of behaviours or of people is far more complicated (see, for example, Angleitner and Demitroder, 1988). What cognitive processes occur in the brain in order to perform such tasks? What kinds of observations are made, and with what frequency, before someone is labelled as being 'sociable' or 'belligerent' or even as 'entre-preneurial'? Does the brain adopt rational or logical principles in order to categorise the behavioural acts (as, for example, in the case of accumulating evidence)? Has it stored within it archetypes by which the observed behaviour can be compared? Does the recognition of patterns of behaviours occur which collectively constitute evidence of the personality disposition? No one knows exactly how the brain works, but it is generally accepted that the performance of such tasks requires the simultaneous consideration of many pieces of information. Each piece may be imperfectly specified or ambiguous yet each may play a decisive role in determining the outcome.

Artificial neural networks are biologically inspired with functions that are reminiscent of human cognition. They have been shown to be applicable to a large class of pattern recognition tasks. These range from applications such as the learning of past tenses of English verbs (Rumelhart and McClelland, 1986) to the detection of explosives in checked airline baggage (Shea and Lin, 1989). They suggest one possible way forward in the search for a method of abstracting patterns from fuzzy and sometimes contradictory data in order to predict the category membership of business owners. Neural networks learn from experience, they generalise and abstract. Their ability to see through noise and distortion to the pattern that lies within and to extract idealised prototypes from imperfect information is particularly apposite to our task.

PLAN OF THIS BOOK

In a monograph of this kind it is possible to set out with various aspirations some of which, like good intentions, fall by the wayside, whereas others assume dominance and shape the character of the work. The single most important purpose we shared was to break out of the mould of prior thinking on the nature of the entrepreneurial personality and to put in its place an alternative research paradigm. However, we were well aware that such a purpose could only be achieved by an awareness of the thoughts and contributions of others who have pondered the depths of this subject before us; by assimilation, reflection and acknowledgement of their views; and by means of this process of reflection to be able to achieve a synthesis of ideas and thereby produce something new.

It has been the aim of this chapter to describe the nature of the problems with which we were faced when we commenced our investigations. We had but a dim view of what might constitute the way forward and had, in fact, strayed along many a blind alley. Our initial sortie was determined; it was to distinguish the various approaches to the subject taken by scholars of different discipline bases (see Chell and Haworth, 1987).

Chapter 2 sets out the variety and to some extent the development of various economists' views of the entrepreneur. This enabled us to bring to bear an historical perspective on the subject. We show that economists are primarily concerned with the function served by entrepreneurs in an economy and that any reference made to aspects of the entrepreneurial personality was of secondary importance. Despite this, mention of two such characteristics tended to recur – the idea of the entrepreneur as a risk-taker and/or as an innovator. Such ideas are traced historically and, for ease of presentation, in the writings of a selection of economists introduced by country of origin. As the analysis is brought up to date, it is clear that some modern economists draw upon psycho-social concepts to develop further their explanations of entrepreneurial behaviour. In sum, this chapter provides a backdrop with which to view the entrepreneur and a, perhaps surprisingly, rich source of ideas regarding their nature.

In chapter 3, the dominant theme is the contribution of the psychologist. The starting point of this chapter is a discussion of what theoretical approach to the conceptualisation of traits should be taken. The Hampsonite view of the construction of personality is put forward. The next section of the chapter examines, in some detail, research which has attempted to demonstrate the centrality of three personality characteristics of entrepreneurs: a need to achieve, an internal locus of control and a propensity to take risks. The equivocal nature of the findings and the use of a variety of implicit definitions of entrepreneur call into question the progress which may be made by continuing to pursue similar lines of enquiry. On the other hand, there have been several attempts to identify a constellation of entrepreneurial characteristics. This avenue is explored as a possible, more fruitful way forward.

Chapter 4 examines the nature of the entrepreneur from sociological and organisational behaviour perspectives. The purpose is chiefly to focus upon the context and consider how those aspects of the business owner's situation shape their actions and behaviour.

The purpose of chapter 5 is to present the methodology which we have adopted for the empirical part of our investigations. The conceptual framework comprises Hampson's constructivist theory of personality which defines traits as categorising concepts. The process of categorisation is central to our methodology and is purported to occur at two levels: (1) the categorisation of behaviour as being prototypical of a particular trait; and, (2) the identification of a set of traits as being prototypical of a particular category of business owner. Operational definitions of four types of owner are presented. In addition, two other dimensions are identified. They are stage of development of the business and growth orientation. Such context- and performance-related measures enable a more detailed classification of business owners. The method of obtaining information was a combination of structured questionnaire and semi-structured interview using a combination of critical incident technique and biographical method. The data obtained were used to prepare the profiles of the thirty-one business owners interviewed. A further methodological issue explored in this chapter was how this qualitative technique of categorisation might be modelled and used for prediction purposes. Artificial neural networks are presented as the way forward.

The collection of very detailed profiles of thirty-one business owners, which were subsequently classified on the three dimensions, enabled the development of detailed case studies. Given the constraints of time and space, five such cases were singled out and they form the content of chapter 6. The cases were purposively selected to highlight the nature of the entrepreneurial personality and only one other category of business owner is represented, that of the quasi-entrepreneur. The cases represent four very different industrial sectors. They also differ in terms of a number of contextual variables including ownership status, level of family involvement, stage of development of the business and age and experience of the owner at founding. The categorisation of these owners and their enterprises is discussed and the supportive evidence of possession of the key attributes is presented.

In chapter 7 the categorisation of the thirty-one business owners on the three dimensions is shown in tabular form. A selection of the profiles of the twenty-six (non-case study) business owners is given in order to demonstrate prototypicality and variation both within and between categories. A further aim is to illustrate how the knowledge gained by the research team, and the methodology adopted, can be used to train a neural network to recognise and predict the category membership of respondents on the basis of their profile on a set of attributes.

Chapter 8 concludes this monograph with a discussion of possible refinements to the methodology and some suggestions for further research in this area.

2 The economists' view of the entrepreneur

In the past, economists have concerned themselves with entrepreneurship which they viewed as the function served by a business person in the economy. Any allusions to the entrepreneurs' personalities were largely incidental. This function has been interpreted in different ways according to whether the particular economist had in mind a dynamic or static view of the economy and whether the entrepreneur was perceived as a force of change. The historical context in which they were writing is important in so far as it is indicative of the issues which were preoccupying them at the time. There are several schools of thought which have emerged and may be labelled according to country of origin. The earliest and most apt statement on the economic function of the entrepreneur came from France. Until the turn of the twentieth century, the British contributed little; at best they ignored the entrepreneur, at worst they confused his role with that of the capitalist. The German and Austrian schools added to the debate, whilst the American school, developed after the Civil War, has made a sustained contribution to our understanding of entrepreneurship, arising from the seminal work of some notable 'emigrés' – Schumpeter being arguably the most well known. Given somewhat limited opportunities for the interchange of ideas, these schools developed their own characteristic approaches.

In this chapter, some of these historical influences are discussed, though there is no pretence at a comprehensive overview. At best such fragments as have been gleaned here give clues as to the variety of views held by economists over the centuries; views on the nature, but more particularly, the function, of the entrepreneur in economic activity. Anticipating the conclusion, current economic thought indicates greater interest in the psychology of the entrepreneur and opens up the possibility of a combined approach whether it be through psychological economics or economic psychology.

AN HISTORICAL PERSPECTIVE

The French school

It is generally accepted that the first economist to recognise the role of the entrepreneur was a Frenchman, Richard Cantillon. In his *Essai* published posthumously in 1755 he described an early market economy in which he distinguished between the role of landowner, entrepreneur and hirelings. Indeed, this tendency to so identify the *dramatis personae* is one of the hallmarks of the classical economists. He suggested that the entrepreneur engages in exchanges for profit and that he is someone who exercises business judgement in the face of uncertainty. Cantillon's analysis raises several issues, the resolution of which is critical to a contemporary understanding of the role of the entrepreneur. They are: the nature of risk and uncertainty facing the entrepreneur *qua* decision-maker; the respective roles of capitalist and entrepreneur in an economy; and the innovative function of the entrepreneur. Cantillon's position on these three critical issues was clear. The uncertainty facing the entrepreneur is of the 'unknowable' kind, by which it is presumed that the entrepreneur cannot calculate the risk with which he is faced in making a decision. Even if the entrepreneur were penniless he does indeed risk something and that is the opportunity cost of pursuing an entrepreneurial venture rather than a safe occupation. The roles of capitalist and entrepreneur are separate. The role of Cantillon's entrepreneur is to be aware of the level of demand and supply but he is not expected to create a demand and in that sense he is not an innovator.

Successive French economists developed further the concept of the entrepreneur. Baudeau (1730–92) injected a sense of the entrepreneur as innovator. His idea was that of a person who invents and applies new techniques in order to reduce his costs and thereby raise his profit (this notion was typical of the so-called 'Physiocrats' at about this time). Certain qualities are needed in order to achieve this; these he identified as ability and intelligence. Through such characteristics, the entrepreneur is able to exert a degree of control over some economic events.

Turgot, a contemporary of Baudeau's, elaborated upon the distinction between capitalist and entrepreneur. The gist of Turgot's idea was that it is the capitalist who has the choice of how he invests his money. If the money is invested in land then he is a capitalist and a landowner. Whilst the capitalist who is an entrepreneur has the function of managing and developing a business, the entrepreneur in this scheme of things is thus distinguished by his labour.

A third Frenchman, Jean-Baptiste Say (1767–1832) helped popularise Cantillon's theory but unlike Cantillon did not see risk or uncertainty as being central to the function of the entrepreneur. Indeed, according to Hébert and Link (1988) Say considered entrepreneurial activity as being virtually synonymous with management.

[The entrepreneur] is called upon to estimate, with tolerable accuracy, the importance of the specific product, the probable amount of the demand, and the means of its production: at one time he must employ a great number of hands; at another, buy or order the raw material, collect labourers, find consumers, and give at all times a rigid attention to order and economy; in a word, he must possess the art of superintendence and administration.

(Say, 1845 edition, quoted in Hébert and Link, 1988, p.38)

However, this may downgrade Say's position. For example, Schumpeter (1961) suggests that Say was the first to afford the entrepreneur a definite position in the economic process. This was to recognise that the role of the entrepreneur is to 'combine the factors of production into a producing organism' (Schumpeter, 1961, p.555). But he did not think that Say's formulation went far enough. It is one thing to combine the factors of production in a firm by taking, as it were, a 'formula approach' and quite another to reorganise such factors in an entirely novel way. Thus it would appear that the problem with Say's formulation is that it detracts attention from a key role of the entrepreneur as a force of change in a dynamic economy.

The British school

The development of the concept of 'entrepreneur' by the French economists progressed in a variety of directions in a less than strict evolutionary sense. Lack of agreement between the French approach and that of the English economists was marked. The entrepreneur as such did not feature prominently in the writings of the British economists during the early eighteenth century. From the time of Adam Smith (1723–90) and the publication of his seminal work *The Wealth of Nations*, the function of entrepreneur was conflated with that of the capitalist; profits were regarded solely as a reward for risking capital. The logic of Smith's argument is clear when it is understood that he was concerned to identify the motives and conditions for the creation of wealth, one such motive being self-interest. Smith's answer to the question: 'Why should a person employ others if no personal benefit is to accrue for so doing?' was unequivocal. Not only might the manufacturer expect to make a profit from his undertaking, but the profit might be expected to bear some relation to the extent of his investment.

> He could have no interest to employ them, unless he expected from the sale of their work something more than what was sufficient to replace his stock to him; and he could have no interest to employ a great stock rather than a small one, unless his profits were to bear some proportion to the extent of his stock.
>
> (Smith, 1976, p.42)

The profits which accrue to the entrepreneur ('undertaker' or 'projector' as they were then called) are not a form of wage arising from the execution of directorial duties. They are a consequence of the level of investment made. In this way Smith equated the function of the entrepreneur with that of the capitalist.

David Ricardo (1772–1823) was an admirer and critic of Adam Smith's work and was also cognisant of the work of Say. However, to all intents and purposes Ricardo and his followers ignored the French tradition. Ricardo expounded the basics of the capitalist system, describing the effect of market forces on the movement of capital. The role of manufacturer is to invest his capital in the business according to demand for his products. If demand falls off then he may 'dismiss some of his workmen and cease to borrow from the bankers and moneyed men. The reverse will be the case where demand increases' (Ricardo, 1962, p.49). In this passage the role of the capitalist is fundamental to the workings of the economy. The manufacturer is a capitalist in so far as he invests in his own business, over and above which his role is one of superintendence. The role of entrepreneur was effectively 'squeezed out' of such an analysis.

Jeremy Bentham (1748–1832) was, until relatively recently, underestimated for his economic writings (Stark, 1952). Bentham's source of inspiration was Adam Smith's *The Wealth of Nations*. But, like his contemporaries, he did not tackle the issue of the nature of the entrepreneur. His theory of production was expounded more with an eye to the role of government. He singled out three key factors which impact upon production. These factors comprised: inclination (the will to produce wealth); the knowledge of how to produce it (in particular technical skill); and power over external things, especially capital and capital goods. He concluded that the government could do little through legislation to affect inclination and knowledge, nor could it do anything about the scarcity of capital. He advocated a *laissez-faire* approach.

A picture of the nineteenth century mill owner as the Industrial Revolution spread throughout England, can be detected in the writings of John Stuart Mill (1806–73). In Book I of his *Principles of Political Economy*, Mill gave the impression of the entrepreneur as a passive capitalist:

> A manufacturer, for example, has one part of his capital in the form of buildings, fitted and destined for carrying on his branch of manufacture. Another part in the form of machinery. A third consists, if he be a spinner, of raw cotton, flax or wool. . . . Each capitalist has money, which he pays to his workpeople, and so enables them to supply themselves; he has also finished goods in his warehouses, by the sale of which he obtains more money, to employ in the same manner, as well as to replenish his stock of raw materials, to keep buildings and machinery in repair, and to replace them when worn out. His money and finished goods, however, are not wholly capital . . . he employs part of the one, and of the proceeds of the other, in supplying his personal consumption and that of his family. . . .
>
> (Mill, 1965, pp.55–6)

One of the concerns of the time, due to the rapid rise in the population, was how to achieve an increase in productivity. Mill (1965) identified the necessary attributes as being the greater energy of labour, superior skill, knowledge, intelligence and trustworthiness. Not everyone, according to Mill, was fitted to direct an industrial enterprise because they lacked the intelligence, but he thought that this could be improved by education.

It is difficult to assess the extent to which Alfred Marshall (1842–1924) was influenced by Charles Darwin's theory of evolution. He espoused the language of evolutionary theory, in particular his references to the survival of the fittest were pointedly applied to the rise and decline of businesses (see for example, Marshall, 1920, p.495). He identified two types of business owner: those who will open out new and improved methods of business and who are unable to avoid taking risks; and those who 'follow beaten tracks' and are given 'wages of superintendence'. To Marshall, business development requires more than mere superintendence of labour; it requires a thorough knowledge of the trade.

> He must have the power of forecasting. . ., of seeing where there is an opportunity for supplying a new commodity that will meet a real want or improving the plan of producing an old commodity. He must be able to judge cautiously and undertake risks boldly; and he must . . . understand the materials and machinery used in his trade. [In addition, he must be] a natural leader of men.
>
> (Marshall, 1920, p.248)

Marshall's undertaker is both alert and innovative:

> the alert businessman strives so to modify his arrangements as to obtain better results with a given expenditure, or equal results with a less expenditure. . . . He pushes the investment of capital in his business in each of several directions until what appears in his judgement to be the outer limit, or margin, of profitableness is reached; that is, until there seems to him no good reason for thinking that the gains resulting from any further investment in that particular direction would compensate him for his outlay.
>
> (*ibid.* pp.295, 298–9).

Business ability is not a scarce resource in so far as everyone has a natural aptitude for it in the conduct of his or her life; it is non-specialised (unlike technical ability and skill) and is identified with the qualities of 'judgment, promptness, resource, carefulness and steadfastness of purpose' (*ibid.* p.503). Further, it would appear that Marshall was beginning to drive a wedge between the notion of capitalist and entrepreneur. In a revealing footnote he quotes Walker:

> [it is] no longer true that a man becomes an employer because he is a capitalist. Men command capital because they have the qualifications to profitably employ labour.
>
> (*ibid.* p.503)

He considered that the job of managing a profitable enterprise comprises two important elements: the mental strain in organising and devising new methods and great anxiety and risk. Profits are the payment for such services and not merely for the job of superintending the business.

Marshall appears to regard the abilities of the successful businessman to be rare. Somewhat graphically, he states that:

> it would be as wasteful if society were to give their work to inferior people who would undertake to do it more cheaply, as it would be to give a valuable diamond to be cut by a low waged but unskilled cutter.

> (*ibid*. p.553)

Marshall developed the concept of 'entrepreneur' relative to the usage of his predecessors, the classical economists, in so far as he thought of entrepreneurs as businessmen who emerged through the evolutionary process of survival of the fittest. Whilst his entrepreneurs were innovative in the sense of devising new methods to reduce costs and therefore produce goods more efficiently, it was left to Schumpeter to develop this notion in a fuller sense. Marshall's successors, Pigou and, his most brilliant student, Keynes added little to the notion of entrepreneur.

The German school

How is the entrepreneur to be compensated for his activity? This was an issue addressed by the German school. The thinking here was predicated on the premise that if entrepreneurial talent is a scarce resource then profit could be regarded as a special kind of payment. In theory, Thunen, (1785–1850) distinguished between the return to the entrepreneur from that of the capitalist by emphasising a residual which is the return to entrepreneurial risk – that risk which is uninsurable. He distinguished between the entrepreneur and manager of an undertaking by suggesting that it is the entrepreneur who takes the problems of the firm home with him. He is the one who has sleepless nights. For Thunen the entrepreneur is both risk-taker and innovator. The return thus comprises the gain or loss associated with an uninsurable risk and entrepreneurial ingenuity *qua* problem solver and innovator.

The issue of risk was extended by refinements suggested by Mangoldt (1824–58). He put forward the now familiar distinction between producing goods to order or for the market so that he could illuminate the relationship between the nature of production and degree of risk. Thus, where a firm produces goods to order it reduces the risk entailed, whereas producing for the market is more speculative given the twin market conditions of uncertain demand and unknown price. He also suggested that the longer the time to final sale, the greater the uncertainty and, conversely, the shorter the time the less the uncertainty and by definition the less entrepreneurial.

Such a distinction may serve to differentiate types of entrepreneur: the former the innovator or inventor, the development of whose product requires a long time scale, the latter the 'opportunistic entrepreneur' who becomes aware of a change in taste and capitalises on that foreseen opportunity. He is nevertheless entrepreneurial in that he has to estimate likely demand whereas the innovator or inventor must create a demand.

The Austrian school

A fourth force in the development of the concept of entrepreneur was that of the Austrian school, its originator being Carl Menger (1840–1921). According to Menger, entrepreneurial activity includes obtaining information about the economic situation. This is because it is the individual's awareness and understanding of the situation which gives rise to economic change. The entrepreneur must make various calculations in order to ensure efficiency of the production process. There must be an act of will to bring about the transformation of higher order goods (for instance, wheat) into lower order goods (for instance, flour) for which there is a market demand and there must be the supervision of the production plan. Throughout this process the entrepreneur faces uncertainty with regard to the quantity and quality of the final goods he can produce. Despite this very clear acknowledgement of the part played by uncertainty, Menger asserted that risk bearing cannot be an essential function of the entrepreneur. In this regard he foreshadowed Schumpeter.

Ludwig von Mises (1881–1972) is identified with the 'Austrian revival'. Defining economics as the study of human action, he put forward the view that human action influences, and is influenced by, the future (Mises, 1949). This aspect of his theory is reminiscent of Shackle. Economic decisions like any other decisions involve making choices and, in addition, coping with future uncertainties. However, his concept of 'entrepreneur' is all embracing.

Indeed, von Mises felt that Schumpeter had confused entrepreneurial activity with technological innovation. The entrepreneur is a decision-taker; making decisions concerning innovative practices are only a part of his sphere of activity. Further, he contended that the profitability (or otherwise) of the enterprise was a consequence of such entrepreneurial acts; it was nothing to do with capitalism. His position on the issue of uncertainty was no different from that of Knight (see the next section).

The American school

The American school began to emerge after the Civil War with a disassociation, by Amasa Walker (1799–1875), from what he viewed as a confusion by the English economists. He recognised the role of the entrepreneur as a creator of wealth whose role should be distinguished from that of the capitalist. His son, Francis A. Walker (1840–97) followed this lead and suggested that the successful conduct of business requires exceptional abilities and opportunities. Successful entrepreneurs have the power of foresight, a facility for organisation and administration, unusual energy and leadership qualities which are generally in short supply. Interestingly he distinguished between four types of entrepreneur: the rare, gifted person, those with high-ordered talent, those that do reasonably well in business, and the ne'er-do-wells. The characteristics he identified with each type are also of interest. The rare, gifted person has the power of foresight, is firm and resolute even in the face of disaster, and is able to motivate and lead others. Persons with a high-ordered talent have a natural mastery; they are wise, prompt and resolute. Those who do reasonably well in business tend to do so through diligence rather than flair or genius, whereas the ne'er-do-wells have perhaps misidentified their vocation and, consequently, they suffer mixed fortunes. This classification conjures up a variety of images of the personality characteristics of business owners and entrepreneurs.

Walker believed that profit is the return to the entrepreneur for his skill, ability or talent. This represented just one view of profit. A theory of profit, as Knight later pointed out, is fundamental to understanding risk and uncertainty (Knight, 1921). In stark contrast, John Bates Clark (1847–1938) put forward the notion of the profitless 'static state'. Clark's theory assumed a static state which itself was assumed to be the 'natural' state of things. The static state is free of all disturbances that progress causes. To realise the static state five kinds of generic change have to be eliminated. These are: (1) population increasing; (2) capital increasing; (3) improving methods of production; (4) change in the forms of industrial establishments; (5) the increase in wants of consumers. In this theoretical state of affairs the cost and selling price are always equal. There can be no profits beyond wages for the routine work of supervision. The prices of these goods are their 'natural price', that is, their 'static price'. Clark argued that profits must arise from a dynamic state. However, these profits are temporary as the forces of competition are always at work to reduce them (Clark, 1907, p.129 *et seq.*). Static state theory has been criticised on two grounds: firstly, that the static state is the 'natural' state and, secondly, that it is change *per se* that is the cause of profit.

Knight (1921) argues that if a change is predictable the result will be neither loss nor profit. Only if the change and its consequences are unforeseen will there be a possibility of profit arising from that change. From this it may be concluded that it is *not* change *per se* but uncertainty which causes profit.

> Without change of some sort there would, it is true, be no profits, for if everything moved along in an absolutely uniform way, the future would be completely foreknown in the present and competition would certainly adjust things to the ideal state where all prices would equal costs.
>
> (Knight, 1921, p.37)

This relationship between profit and the assumption of risk was pursued by a contemporary of Clark – F.B. Hawley (1843–1929). In Hawley's distributive theory profit is the reward to the entrepreneur for assuming risk. If there was no such inducement there would be no reason for the entrepreneur to embark on risky ventures. Hawley, however, did not distinguish between insurable and non-insurable risk. It was Knight who later attempted to reconcile these two theories on the grounds that profit is bound up with economic change (because change is a condition of uncertainty) and profit is a result of risk which cannot be measured.

The issues of risk and uncertainty received considerable prominence at the turn of the century. Whilst for some (for example, Hawley) a business transaction is carried out in conditions of uncertainty *à la* Cantillon, for others (for example Clark, Davenport and later, Schumpeter) risk bearing was not an entrepreneurial activity. Frank Knight added further clarification by distinguishing between insurable risks (based on statistical probability) and uninsurable uncertainty. He put forward a theory of profit which related non-insurable uncertainty to rapid economic change and to differences in entrepreneurial ability. He argued that in situations of risk it was possible to assign a probability estimate to the likely occurrence of an event. Whereas, in the cases of true uncertainty no such assignment can be made; the situation is unique. In such cases, all that can be done is to make a judgement as to what should be done. There is no sense in which the individual can calculate the probability that he is wrong.

A refinement of Knight's distinction suggests that there are three states of risk/uncertainty. They are: (1) risk in the sense of a probability distribution of possible outcomes which are calculable and known; (2) uncertainty where the possible outcomes are listable but the probability distribution is unknown; and (3) radical uncertainty where the possible outcomes are unknown and unlistable (Hébert and Link, 1988). However, Knight's distinction between a probable outcome and an uncertain outcome has been questioned on the grounds that from the stance of the entrepreneur the probable outcome is ultimately a subjective probability. Whilst he may have more *confidence* in his judgement in such cases it does not obviate the fact that he is still operating in conditions of uncertainty.

Knight's theory of uncertainty helps establish the boundary between the manager and the entrepreneur: a manager becomes an entrepreneur when the exercise of his judgement is liable to error and he assumes the responsibility for its correctness. Thus, he suggests that the characteristics possessed by individuals who are able to direct others in conditions of uncertainty are: (1) knowledge and judgement; (2) foresight; (3) superior managerial ability; (4) confidence in their judgement. Entrepreneurial income comprises two parts: a wage or rent element for his abilities and payment for uncertainty bearing.

All the theories of entrepreneurship outlined to this point assumed an entrepreneur who responded to an outside force which impacted upon the market system. Joseph Schumpeter, in contrast, suggested that the entrepreneur is a dynamic, proactive force – an endogenous factor. Schumpeter is the architect of a theory of economic development in which the entrepreneur is central; the entrepreneur's role is to disturb the economic status quo through innovations. Development is a process defined by the carrying out of new combinations of factors of production. The entrepreneur innovates and thereby creates these 'new combinations'. Innovations may be of various sorts according to Schumpeter. They may result from:

- the creation of a new product or alteration in its quality;
- the development of a new method of production;
- the opening of a new market;
- the capture of a new source of supply;
- a new organisation of industry.

Everyone is an entrepreneur only when he actually 'carries out new combinations,' and loses that character as soon as he has built up his business, when he settles down to running it as other people run their businesses.

(Schumpeter, 1934, p.78)

This kind of innovation assumes a depth of understanding of an industry, including technological and product market knowledge, and also leadership ability.

Schumpeter's position was that entrepreneurial profits may be separated from the earnings of management. Profit is a residual, a surplus. A surplus may arise due to an innovative act by the entrepreneur which has resulted in lowering costs or raising the value of the product or service. The size of the surplus is directly attributable to the entrepreneur's productivity. In this way, it is possible to see how Schumpeter arrived at the conclusion that profit is not a return to risk. Risk falls on the capitalist not the entrepreneur *qua* entrepreneur. This suggests that profit is both the price and the payment for the services rendered by the entrepreneur.

CONTEMPORARY INFLUENCES

Theoretical developments after Schumpeter lead us to the present day. Some notable contributions are those of G.L.S. Shackle, Israel Kirzner, Mark Casson and T.W. Schultz. A marked characteristic of all these economic theorists is their recognition of the need to introduce psychological concepts into an economic account of entrepreneurial behaviour.

Shackle's concern is with the psychic act of decision making in conditions of bounded uncertainty. He theorises that an entrepreneur, like an artist, is an 'originator'. The entrepreneur imbues his sense impressions with meaning and through this act of imagination he perceives the potential of the situations and resources at his disposal and characteristically gambles on his imagination.

Israel Kirzner, a student of von Mises, followed a different tack:

he defined entrepreneurship as 'alertness to profit opportunities'. The psychological aspect of such a definition is that it is based on individual differences in perception. He distinguishes between the arbitrageur and the entrepreneur on the grounds that only in the latter case is there a need for acts of creative imagination in the face of uncertainty; the former is rather more a case of adjusting prices and costs in the light of experience.

Kirzner explains the value of entrepreneurship as a 'corrective' to unexploited profit opportunities arising from the misallocation of resources which result in 'social waste'. Such a misallocation, he argues, arises from imperfect knowledge, but this knowledge has to do with awareness rather than the gathering of information which indicates a subtle difference between his position and that of Schultz.

> Entrepreneurial profit opportunities exist where people do not know what they do not know, and do not know that they do not know it. The entrepreneurial function is to notice what people have overlooked.
>
> (Kirzner, 1982, p.273)

Casson (1982), whilst pursuing a slightly different line of enquiry, also draws upon psychological concepts in his account of what constitutes entrepreneurial behaviour. Indeed, he considers the integration of the functional and the indicative approaches to be a primary purpose of his work. He presents the idea that an entrepreneur is someone who specialises in taking judgemental decisions about the coordination of scarce resources (*ibid*. p.23). The notion of the judgemental decision is central. It is a decision 'where different individuals, sharing the same objectives and acting under similar circumstances, would make different decisions' (*ibid*. p.24). They would make different decisions because they have 'different perceptions of the situation' as a result of different information or interpretation. The entrepreneur is therefore a person whose judgement differs from that of others. His reward arises from his backing his judgement and being right. The term 'coordination' Casson defines as the 'beneficial reallocation of resources'; a dynamic concept intended to capture the entrepreneur as an agent of change. This assumption that coordination is beneficial may be criticised if it is intended to indicate a key characteristic of entrepreneurs. Whilst it is accepted that the entrepreneur may choose to reallocate resources, allowance must be made for the fact that on occasions he fails to do this beneficially, otherwise 'success' is implicit in his definition of 'entrepreneur'.

A further adjunct to the theory is the exposition of the qualities associated with the entrepreneur. Casson (1982) argues that the successful entrepreneur must generally be proficient in all aspects of decision-making (unless he is to delegate). The qualities of imagination and foresight are scarce and so the possession of them confers an advantage. He discusses all these skills in terms of whether they are innate, scarce, difficult to screen for, and/or likely to be enhanced through experience or training. This particular analysis is an example of psychological economics and its accuracy is an empirical question.

Schultz (1980), a pioneer of human capital theory, has attempted to broaden the concept of entrepreneurship by suggesting that, in a dynamic economy, entrepreneurial behaviour may be manifested by people other than those in business. Such behaviour is a function of the demand, supply and value of their services. At any point in a person's lifecycle he or she may, due to changes in economic circumstances, become entrepreneurial. Entrepreneurial ability is the 'ability to reallocate their services in response to changes in the value of the work they do' (*ibid.* p.441). In this sense some educational activities can be considered to be entrepreneurial. It is the supply of entrepreneurial ability which is of economic value but which has received scant consideration in the economic literature. Given that what they do has economic value, this value accrues to them as rent. Further, Schultz argues strongly that risk-bearing is not a unique attribute of the entrepreneur. Even in a static economy there is risk, but there are no entrepreneurs. He concludes that the bearing of risk does not distinguish between people who are entrepreneurs and those who are not. In essence, the entrepreneurial reward is solely for their ability and not as a consequence of their taking risks.

The decision to reallocate resources rests on current information and expectations based on that information. This implies a need to keep constantly up to date. The more able the entrepreneur the more efficient he is likely to be in acquiring and acting upon information. Schultz believes that education has an effect on people's ability to perceive and react to disequilibria. For example, in farming the entrepreneur can, through education, increase his understanding of new agricultural techniques and so gain a competitive advantage.

HÉBERT AND LINK'S TAXONOMY OF ENTREPRENEURIAL THEORIES

In their historical exegesis of economic thought, Hébert and Link (1988) have attempted a taxonomy of entrepreneurial theories, for which they have the following twelve themes:

1 The entrepreneur is the person who assumes the risk associated with uncertainty*.
2 The entrepreneur is the person who supplies financial capital.
3 The entrepreneur is an innovator*.
4 The entrepreneur is a decision-maker*.
5 The entrepreneur is an industrial leader*.
6 The entrepreneur is a manager or superintendent.
7 The entrepreneur is an organiser and coordinator of economic resources*.
8 The entrepreneur is the owner of an enterprise.
9 The entrepreneur is an employer of factors of production.
10 The entrepreneur is a contractor*.
11 The entrepreneur is an arbitrageur*.
12 The entrepreneur is an allocator of resources among alternative uses*.

At least one, and usually several of the themes have been advocated by different economic theorists. Hébert and Link explain that, whilst theories of entrepreneurship may be static or dynamic, only the latter have 'any significant operational meaning' (*ibid*. p.153). Those themes which accommodate the dynamic approach are signified thus '*'. Albeit simplified, these authors feel able to identify three major intellectual traditions with their roots in Cantillon. These they label as:

- The Chicago tradition – Knight–Schultz.
- The German tradition – Thunen–Schumpeter.
- The Austrian tradition – Mises–Kirzner–(Shackle).

These traditions share various themes in common; those of perception, uncertainty and innovation (or other special abilities). They have all emphasised the *function* of the entrepreneur as opposed to his or her *personality*. His role as a dynamic force is to restore equilibrium in a market economy.

In an attempt at synthesis, Hébert and Link put forward the following definition of 'entrepreneur':

[The entrepreneur is] someone who specialises in taking responsibility for and making judgemental decisions that affect the location, the form, and the use of goods, resources, or institutions.

(Hébert and Link, 1988, p.155)

Their elaboration of this definition is worthy of note. They suggest that it contains the notions of risk, uncertainty, innovation, perception and change:

This person [the entrepreneur] has a comparative advantage in decision making, and makes decisions that run counter to the conventional wisdom either because he/she has better information or a better perception of events or opportunities. . . . The entrepreneur must have the courage of his/her convictions and face the consequences of his/her actions, whether they produce profits or losses. Entrepreneurial activities are performed . . . by individuals whose judgement differs from the norm.

(Hébert and Link, 1988, p.155)

On the issue of uncertainty they point out that 'uncertainty is a consequence of change, whereas innovation is a precept of change' (*ibid*. p.156). The distinction between the roles of entrepreneur and capitalist is also now much clearer: for example, true entrepreneurial gains bear no relation to the size of capital employed in a business. However, one thing that the entrepreneur and capitalist have in common is that they both face an element of risk. Finally, the question of whether the entrepreneur is the person who instigates change or merely adjusts to it is raised. Hébert and Link believe that it does not matter: either reaction requires perception, courage and action; failure in any of these departments will render the entrepreneur ineffective.

CONCLUDING STATEMENT

This very brief survey of economic thought on the question of the function of the entrepreneur in an economy has demonstrated:

1 A gradual and increasing awareness of the crucial role played by entrepreneurs in economic growth.
2 A theoretical contradiction between equilibrium theory and the disruptive function of the entrepreneur, that is, a person who deals in conditions of disequilibria.

3   The very different traditions and treatments of the entre-
    preneur, with a strong British tradition which minimised his
    role and supplanted it with that of the capitalist.
4   An initial preoccupation with risk taking and decision taking in
    conditions of uncertainty as being fundamental to the behaviour
    of the entrepreneur. This, as a key characteristic of entre-
    preneurs, has since been questioned.
5   Various approaches to explain the entrepreneur's motivation
    though they all may be boiled down to the profit motive; to
    'buy cheap and sell dear', to exploit a profit opportunity, to be
    aware of new developments in technology in order to reduce
    the costs of production and gain a competitive advantage.
6   The recognition of various psychological and behavioural
    characteristics of entrepreneurs which distinguish them from
    other business owners. Such characteristics have included
    foresight, a keen awareness of possibilities, a creative imagina-
    tion, confidence in their decision (that is, a willingness to
    gamble on their imagination) and being an agent of change. The
    entrepreneur is not simply an overseer, a superintendent or a
    'caretaker', he actively pursues and initiates change. This has
    been taken to mean, by some, that he is an innovator in so far
    as the pursuit of change was not change for change's sake. In
    the Schumpeterian sense, he might develop new products,
    exploit new markets, introduce new technologies, capture a
    new source of supply, use imaginative ways of investing in the
    business, reorganise systems and structures to accomplish
    efficiencies in operations and/or bring about the reshaping of an
    industrial sector.

The economists have also indicated where the boundary lies
between their own approach to understanding the function of the
entrepreneur and that of other discipline bases. Of principal concern
is the ability to develop an understanding of the nature of
entrepreneurs and entrepreneurship from a psychological perspective. This will be the task of ensuing chapters.

NOTE

The interested reader who might wish to delve deeper into the
earlier usage and historical origins of the term 'entrepreneur' should
consult R.E. Hébert and A.N. Link (1988) *The Entrepreneur –
mainstream views and radical critiques*, 2nd edition, New York:
Praeger.

3 The search for entrepreneurial traits

When a proportion of the business community distinguish themselves by their entrepreneurial flair then the inference that such people must share some characteristic in common is not a surprising one. Such a conclusion has led researchers to make many attempts to identify a set of traits which distinguish entrepreneurs from other business men and women (see reviews in Brockhaus, 1982; Brockhaus and Horwitz, 1986; Chell, 1985; Chell and Haworth, 1988). Several candidates have been put forward but the evidence has tended to be contradictory.

In this chapter an attempt is made to take a fresh look at the problem. First of all, personality theory is examined; the idea of personality 'traits' as residing *within* the individual is questioned and an alternative, social psychological theory of personality is put forward. Secondly, a critical appraisal of research which followed a univariate approach is presented. A number of methodological problems are identified which may have contributed to the equivocal research results. In the third section, two studies which have attempted to identify a profile of characteristics which typify *successful* entrepreneurs are described. Finally, the issues raised by the work outlined in the chapter as a whole are discussed.

THE RELEVANCE OF PERSONALITY THEORY

There is a problem which is more fundamental than the empirical work of identifying entrepreneurial characteristics. It is to arrive at an understanding of the nature of personality in general, given the considerable revisions in thinking that have taken place in recent years. This revision may be said to have commenced with an attack on the 'traditional' trait approach launched by Mischel (1968, 1973).

29

In its original form, traits such as sociable, anxious, energetic, etc. were thought to exist within the individual to whom they were applied. Further, trait theory assumed that people not only behave in the same way in the same (or similar) situations, but that they should behave similarly across a range of situations. Mischel's line of criticism lay in questioning this assumption. Hampson (1982, 1988) has documented the evidence and outlined key issues in the debate which then ensued.

The debate was a contest between the supremacy of the personality theorists' versus the social psychologists' explanations of behaviour. Trait theory came under considerable attack and an alternative theory of personality known as *interactionism* was put forward. This theory explicitly allowed for the influence of situations or social contexts on behaviour. It has had many advocates and empirical evidence has accumulated to substantiate it (see, for example, Argyle and Little, 1972; Endler and Magnusson, 1976; Magnusson, 1981). The idea was that behaviour was shaped by personality, the situation *and* their interaction.

This theory looked promising but the criticisms of it call into question its utility. These criticisms are largely methodological. For example, an immediate problem is the need to document the relevant dimensions of situations which conceivably affect the target person's behaviour. A further problem is the identification and measurement of interaction effects. Even in a laboratory situation such effects may be difficult to replicate for there is always the possibility of the moderating effects of another variable. A third criticism is that interactionism still gives personality traits a key explanatory role without resolving the problem of behavioural consistency.

The search for alternative methodologies has fuelled the debate throughout the 1980s. One attempt to develop a fundamental shift in personality theory and to redirect attention to a novel methodology is that of Hampson's theory of the construction of personality (Hampson, 1982, 1988). The constructivist approach, as she terms it, is an attempt to take into consideration three perspectives on personality – the personality theorist's, the lay, and the self-perspectives. The personality theorist's perspective assumes an *explicit theory* of personality, that is, an attempt is made to describe what personality is by inferring the structure of personality from observations of behaviour. In contrast, the lay perspective assumes an *implicit theory* of personality, which comprises descriptive and intuitive beliefs which reside in people's minds. People have theories about their own personalities which act as a guide and enable them to manipulate and control other people through impression management. The self-perspective assumes the existence of *self* constructs. Further, there are reciprocal influences of other people's perception of one's self. Awareness of these perceptions in turn affect one's own perception of one's self and this, consequently, affects how one projects one's self to others.

Hampson argues that the personality theorist has shown no interest in either lay views about personality or in the beliefs which subjects hold about themselves. Moreover, there is an assumption of objectivity about the way personality theorists conduct their investigations which apparently does not stand up to close examination:

> The investigation of explicit personality is intended to be the objective measurement of inferred, underlying psychological properties of individuals. However, the claimed independence of the study of explicit personality from the lay and self perspectives does not stand up to close examination. Lay beliefs influence the choice of constructs to be studied and the way they are measured.
>
> (Hampson, 1988, pp.192–3)

A key issue is how the personality theorist decides which personality constructs to study. Hampson argues that these constructs largely have their origins in lay beliefs. The preparation of the psychological inventory which has been assumed to be an objective systematic exercise is also criticised. It is suggested that the test designer relies upon his or her knowledge and beliefs about behaviour–trait relations in composing many questionnaire items. Hampson gives her own examples of where assumptions about the behaviour purported to be indicative of the construct have subsequently been shown to be erroneous. The following quotation, not one of Hampson's examples, illustrates this point and the more general one of the extent to which the test designer uses his or her own judgement in devising a personality inventory.

> 'Do you let your dog lick your face?' This item was intended to tap cleanliness and was keyed No. Obviously those without dogs would endorse No, it was argued, but cleanliness was often a reason for not owning pets. To my surprise, this item provoked an exceedingly powerful response. Some individuals on coming on this item actually abandoned the test trial saying that the whole

thing was disgusting: one subject even told me he had never been so insulted, that he would never allow so filthy an act, and so on in that vein.

(Kline, 1986, p.65)

Hampson (1988) concludes that:

the assessment of psychological equivalence of behaviours should be conducted prior to the empirical investigation of behavioural consistency and should take account of the lay and self perspectives.

(Hampson, 1988, p.194)

Research has shown that people share a common understanding of the behaviours they believe to be associated with traits and also the co-occurrence relations between traits. For example, it might be expected that people who are sociable are more likely to be helpful. The traits 'sociable' and 'helpful' being believed to co-occur, Hampson goes on to demonstrate that the psychologists' explicit theories and the implicit theories of the lay person have much in common. However, she then goes on to argue a very controversial point (see, for example, Kenrick and Funder, 1988), that 'personality does not have an *objective* existence independent of the human observer' (Hampson, 1988, p.195). Behaviour is only understood as being socially meaningful once it has been *categorised* and *interpreted*.

In sum, the personality theorist is solely concerned with the individual or actor, with an attempt to measure the characteristics which that person brings to a situation. The observer's contribution, that is, how the actor's behaviour is perceived and *construed* by others is ignored, so too is the actor's own perceptions or awareness of him or herself.

Hampson (1984) addresses the issue of what she regards as a false dichotomy between the 'real' and the 'perceived' personality. Personality theorists regard personality as 'a set of characteristics which may be said to be *within* the individual causing her or him to behave in certain ways' (p.29). They are attempting to come to grips with the 'real' personality, whereas person perception is only concerned with people's *beliefs* about real personality. But is there an overlap between perceived and actual personality or is the former a gross distortion of actual personality?

Evidence has been adduced to suggest that *both* ratings of 'real' personality and of 'perceived' personality may be dismissed as figments of the imagination (Mischel, 1968; D'Andrade, 1974; Shweder, 1975, 1977; Shweder and D'Andrade, 1979). The problem is that personality may only be inferred; there is no true objective measure of personality.

> All rating scales vary with respect to the degree to which they refer to specific behavioural acts or require inference from a general impression. . . . [Therefore] personality ratings even when taken under optimum on-the-spot conditions involving specific concrete behaviours, are inevitably a representation of reality that has been filtered through the human information processing system. . . . There can never be truly objective ratings because ratings are more than just frequency counts of actual behaviours. . . . A personality rating . . . involves the rater distinguishing certain events in the behaviour stream and drawing inferences from these events to a more abstract concept.
>
> (Hampson, 1984, pp.33–4)

This does not mean that perceived personality is merely a reflection of the similarity in meanings between personality terms used as labels on the rating scales. If it were, raters would be insensitive to the inconsistencies between the characteristics of the ratees and the semantic similarity between the rating scales. *Immediate* ratings have been shown not to accord with semantic similarity beliefs. Hampson concludes that the distinction between actual and perceived personality is in effect meaningless: 'A personality rating is the product of a constructive filter which imposes structure on what is seen' (*ibid*. p.35). Rather than personality being thought to reside *within* individuals, she suggests it may be located metaphorically *between* them.

What then do 'traits' refer to?

> Traits are categories for social behaviour, and these categories only have meaning in so far as they have generally recognised social significance. We. . . share a common set of understandings about the meaning of social behaviour; personality traits are used as a way of summarising and communicating this meaning.
>
> (Hampson, 1984, p.38)

Just as the manifestations of objects such as 'birds' are clusters of co-occurring attributes such as feathers, beak, wings then traits may be regarded as semantic categories 'referring to clusters of co-occurring behavioural and situational attributes' (*ibid*.). Hampson's constructivist theory thus assumes that traits are based on actual behaviour which is perceived by observers and categorised in trait terms. The distinction between actual and perceived personality collapses as the trait categorisation of socially constructed personality replaces the idea of perceived real-world behaviour. This means that a different approach is needed to investigate personality traits:

> Socially-constructed personality traits are assumed to be anchored in the real world, in the sense that they are used as categories to apply to perceived behaviour. Of course, observations of behaviour are never truly objective, but are *perceptions* and therefore open to the influence of the perceiver's information processing system. . . For the constructivist position, evidence is required that observers are capable of perceiving patterns of behaviour on which to base the personality construction process. These patterns must 'exist' in so far as the trait labels applied to them are useful for communicative and predictive purposes. Thus the constructivist view is supported by evidence of behavioural consistency derived from observations of behaviour.
>
> (Hampson, 1984, pp.38–9)

As individuals, people share 'common understandings' to some degree. But there are multiple perspectives and interpretations of social behaviours and as such different perceivers might adopt different interpretations. Through discussion a *social* consensus may be arrived at. In order to do this the self-perspective may be crucial in so far as consideration is given to the individual's account of their own behaviour. Social interaction is a process of negotiation of situations and social encounters. The categorisation of behaviour and conclusions about the nature of an individual's personality is a consequence of this process.

A practical problem in terms of lay perceptions of personality is that people may make trait attributions on the basis of scant evidence and therefore may arrive at biased judgements as to the nature of the personality in question. On the other hand, psychologists using a single measure of a personality dimension may also be over-confident about the conclusions they draw with respect to the nature of personality. Ideally, multiple observations across a variety of situations conducted by more than one person are required to begin to measure the consistent nature of any one individual's personality (Kenrick and Funder, 1988).

A key implication of this theory is the criticism of the

methodology of psychometric measurement using personality inventories. In essence, by making the lay theory explicit it is possible to devise new methods of assessing personality traits. The idea that traits operate like categorising concepts (personality-descriptive nouns or adjectives) may be taken as the key to this new methodology.

Prototypicality

The basis of Hampson's methodology is the work of Rosch and her colleagues who have put forward a model of semantic categories for objects (Rosch *et al.* 1976). The appeal of this work is that it is based on real-world knowledge. It assumes that criteria for category inclusion are imprecise and as such it incorporates the Wittgensteinian notion of 'family resemblance' (Rosch, 1978). In other words, most categories do not have clear-cut boundaries and so the idea that it is possible to devise a set of necessary and sufficient criteria for category membership is problematic. Categories may be conceived of in terms of clear cases which typify them rather than in terms of their boundaries. Essentially this is to seek 'prototypical cases' of a category. The prototype is the best exemplar of a particular category. For example, a mahogany dining table is more prototypical of the category 'table' than is a desk. However, as Hampson points out:

> Variations in prototypicality come about because membership of object categories is not an all-or-none affair; instead it depends on an object possessing a greater number of the distinguishing features of one category than those of another.
>
> (Hampson, 1982, p.165)

For example, a patio window (or a patio door!) has many of the attributes of both the 'window' category and the 'door' category and is difficult to categorise and therefore not prototypical of either category.

Cantor and Mischel (1979) have applied Rosch's framework to the categorisation of people. A primary concern was to develop further an understanding of the function which categories serve in the perceptual process. These researchers drew a very strong analogy between object categorisation à la Rosch and person categorisation. Person categories may also be described as 'fuzzy sets' (i.e. have ill-defined boundaries) which are best exemplified by the use of prototypical cases. Specific person categories used by these researchers to illustrate their point are the extroverted person, the cultured person, the person committed to a belief or cause and the emotionally unstable person. These are noun phrases and some of the concepts adopted were not in everyday use. Their work highlighted the distinction between personality nouns (from which one might arrive at a typology of people) and traits. Whilst nouns categorise people, traits categorise behaviours (Hampson, 1988). Hampson's work has been to extend the Rosch model to traits (Hampson, 1982; Hampson, *et al.*, 1986). Thus behaviours may be assigned to a trait category on the basis of their prototypicality.

The main conclusion to be drawn from Hampson's work is that personality can no longer be viewed as residing exclusively within the individual, it is also a product of social processes resulting from observer and self-observer perspectives. The implications of this theory for future work purporting to measure personality need to be fully explored.

CRITIQUE OF THE TRAIT APPROACH AS APPLIED TO THE ENTREPRENEUR

In the previous section the constructivist theory of personality was outlined. However, this theoretical approach has not been applied to the entrepreneurial personality. Attempts to identify and measure the personality traits of the 'entrepreneur' using conventional psychological techniques have been roundly criticised (Stevenson and Sahlman, 1989). This section presents an overview of such criticisms.

> At the heart of the matter is whether the psychological and social traits are either necessary or sufficient for the development of entrepreneurship. Character traits are at best modalities and not universalities, since many successful and unsuccessful entrepreneurs do not share the characteristics identified. Further, historical studies do not show the same character traits in earlier entrepreneurs. Also, the studies of life paths of entrepreneurs often show decreasing 'entrepreneurship' following success. Such evidence at least raises a question whether the nature of entrepreneurship is immutably embedded in the personality from early stages of childhood development. Finally, while many authors have purported to find statistically significant common characteristics of entrepreneurs, the ability to attribute causality to these factors is seriously in doubt.
>
> (Stevenson and Sahlman, 1989, pp.103–4)

This indictment gains further credence when one considers that the research findings on entrepreneurial traits have yielded equivocal results. Different schools of thought have offered explanations of entrepreneurial behaviour, but there seems to be little agreement regarding the profile of the entrepreneur. From the psychological literature, entrepreneurs were thought to be moderate risk-takers (as discussed in Meredith *et al.*, 1982), deviants (Kets de Vries, 1977), high in need for achievement (McClelland, 1961, 1965), and to have an internal locus of control (Brockhaus, 1982) and a tolerance of ambiguity (Schere, 1982). More recently, the characteristic of a Type A behaviour pattern has been identified as a promising indicator for differentiating entrepreneurs from managers (Boyd, 1984; Begley and Boyd, 1985). The Type A construct is intended to measure the degree to which a respondent displays extremes of competitiveness, aggressiveness, impatience, striving for achievement and feelings of being under pressure.

Some of the differences may, in part, be due to the differing definitions of 'entrepreneur' used in these studies, the inadequacy of the research design and the measuring instruments. Notwithstanding such criticisms, it is important that such work be considered and not dismissed out of hand. To this end, the literature on three personality dimensions: need for achievement, locus of control and risk-taking – as applied to the entrepreneur – is reviewed below.

Need for achievement

The work of McClelland, in the early to mid-1960s, suggested that the key to entrepreneurial behaviour lies in achievement motivation. The need to achieve is a drive to excel, to achieve a goal in relation to a set of standards. A person endowed with such a need will spend time considering how to do a job better or how to accomplish something important to them. McClelland distinguished this type of person from the rest, suggesting they were 'high achievers'. High achievers are said to like situations where they can take personal responsibility for finding solutions to problems. They like rapid feedback on their performance so that they can judge whether they are improving or not. They avoid what they perceive to be very easy or very difficult tasks and they dislike succeeding by chance. They prefer striving to achieve targets which present both a challenge and are not beyond their capabilities. This ensures worthwhile effort and results in feelings of accomplishment and satisfaction.

McClelland's theory, which was developed with greater mathematical precision by Atkinson (Atkinson and Birch 1979), has been criticised on methodological grounds, for example, in his extensive use of the Thematic Apperception Test (Sexton and Bowman, 1984). Furthermore, the predictive power of McClelland's theory is questionable. Brockhaus (1982) has pointed out that McClelland's empirical research did not directly connect need for achievement (nAch) with the decision to own and manage a business. This problem is corroborated by the findings of Hull *et al.* (1980) who found nAch to be a weak predictor of an individual's tendency to start a business. A relationship so described may, in fact, only serve to obscure the operation of the achievement motive. The reasons why people start their own business have been shown to be a mixture of 'push' and 'pull' factors which may be or may not be associated with the need to achieve. Given that there are a variety of reasons for setting up in business, it follows that business owners will vary in their motivational structure from those who enjoy a challenge to the person who has sought self-employment as a more desirable form of earning a living – an alternative lifestyle perhaps.

Other criticisms relate to McClelland's attempt to relate economic development to the prevalence of achievement imagery (Wilken, 1979). The cultural basis of the achievement motive and its effects are open to speculation. For example, historically the British culture was such that its 'high achievers' were 'creamed off' for top jobs in administration and government. Self-employment was not regarded as an attractive option until the popularisation of the 'enterprise culture' in the Thatcher era of the 1980s. This British attitude towards self-employment together with the stigma attached to business failure is not evident in the United States, for instance, where failure is seen as a positive learning experience.

McClelland's theory also includes the idea that the achievement motive can be inculcated through socialisation and training. Such work has been carried out in several Third World countries, including India, Malawi and Ecuador. In the UK, attitudes towards the training and development of entrepreneurial aspirations and behaviours may be shifting as the impact of various enterprise programmes introduced into the educational system begins to take effect.

Despite these criticisms there is some empirical support for the idea that entrepreneurs have a higher motive to achieve than people in general, for example, Hornaday and Aboud, (1971) and Begley and Boyd, (1986), none of whom used the Thematic Apperception

Test. Even if achievement motivation exists as a stable characteristic and is consistently found to be more prevalent amongst entrepreneurs (as opposed to business owners generally) there is still a question of its relation to business performance. McClelland has confirmed that training courses designed to develop achievement motivation have improved small business performance significantly in terms of increased sales, profits and numbers employed (McClelland and Winter, 1971; Miron and McClelland, 1979). More recently, he has addressed the question as to whether there are other key personal characteristics needed for entrepreneurial success (McClelland, 1987). A critical issue in research is whether such findings can be replicated. Begley and Boyd (1986) found very little relationship between various psychological characteristics of founders and non-founders and measures of business performance.

In sum, such a body of work raises questions with respect to the centrality of the achievement motive as a characteristic of entrepreneurs. Despite the claims of empirical support, there are lingering doubts as to the predictive power of the achievement motive.

Locus of control

Rotter (1966) developed the notion of 'locus of control of reinforcement' as part of a wider social learning theory of personality. People with an *internal* locus of control are those individuals who believe themselves to be in control of their destiny. In contrast, people with an *external* locus of control sense that fate, in the form of chance events outside their control or powerful people, has a dominating influence over their lives (Levenson, 1973). Given this very generalised sense of a locus of control it might be expected that most business owners, have a higher internal locus of control than the population at large. After all, it is the nature of the management process that control be exerted over those factors which they identify as having an influence on their business. Indeed, this reasoning may be applied to chief executive officers, senior management and so on. It is perhaps not surprising, therefore, that one study reported that no evidence had been found to distinguish between business founders (whom the researchers equated to entrepreneurs) and non-founders (equated to business managers) (Begley and Boyd, 1986).

Another line of enquiry which has been investigated is the relationship between need for achievement (nAch) and locus of control. It would seem logical to suppose, as did Rotter (1966), that these two characteristics should be positively related. That is, people who have high nAch believe in their own ability to control the outcome of their efforts. Borland (1974) (as cited in Brockhaus, 1982) suggests that a belief in internal locus of control was a better predictor of entrepreneurial intentions than nAch. Hull *et al.* (1980) disagree with Borland in that they failed to find a relationship between locus of control scores and entrepreneurial activity, but do agree that nAch is not the most important variable. To complicate the issue further, Brockhaus and Nord (1979) found that internal locus of control scores failed to distinguish between entrepreneurs and managers. On the other hand, a study by Brockhaus (1980a) shows promise for distinguishing between successful and unsuccessful founders. The criterion of success was that the business still existed three years after the locus of control scores were obtained. The founders of the 'successful' businesses had a higher internal locus of control than the founders of those businesses which had subsequently ceased to exist.

What should one conclude from such conflicting evidence? There are two possible ways forward which we will consider. One is to examine critically the use of a locus of control scale for measuring this trait. The alternative is to question fundamentally whether locus of control is a key distinguishing characteristic of entrepreneurs and is not part of a wider, more generalisable orientation to the business. This issue is in part to do with the utility of using a psychometric measure which has not been specifically designed for populations of business owners.

Furnham (1986) has indicated a fundamental weakness in the locus of control scale as developed by Rotter (1966); that is, its unidimensionality. It would appear that people view the effects of chance and of powerful others differently. Further, different researchers have applied the locus of control measure to a variety of settings: health, religious beliefs, education, political behaviour and behaviour in organisations. In the latter case, researchers have used or adapted generalised locus of control scales rather than attempting to modify or adapt the concept to economic or organisational issues. For this reason, Furnham (1986) has developed and tested his own economic locus of control scale. He demonstrated that this scale was multidimensional, the dimensions being internality, chance, external-denial and powerful others. He was also able to demonstrate clear differences in response according to a number of demographic variables: sex, age, education, voting behaviour and income. A possible extension might be to target the population of business owners and control for such variables as size and age of firm, industrial sector and location taking into account local labour market conditions.

How do business owners view factors associated with locus of control? Some business environments are very turbulent, some industrial sectors are more competitive than others, whilst business owners vary with respect to their preference for constant change or relative stability. Fluctuations in the performance of a firm give a temporal dimension which may at any single point in time influence the business owners' sense of control. Moreover, what does it really mean for a business owner to have scored in a particular way on a measure of locus of control and how reliable are those data? How does locus of control relate to other business behaviours, such as confidence, decisiveness, quality of judgement, business success, etc.? Such information cannot be gathered by means of personality scales.

The complex nature of such behaviour may be addressed by examining a hypothetical example of the business owner's behaviour. In a business situation, the cognitive process of developing and implementing plans and strategies in an effort to steer the business along a successful course is a specific instance of an individual's attempt to control and manage the environment. The strategy is designed to create a situation where the odds of 'winning' are weighed in his or her favour. In exercising judgement and attempting to be 'realistic', the business owner is likely to be aware of the power of situations and of other people, whilst simultaneously trying to reduce their influence. This suggests that in a business context, behaviour associated with judgemental decision-making needs to be taken into account. Such behaviour may be viewed in relation to performance outcomes. It is not unusual for business owners to suffer setbacks or occasionally experience business failure. It is likely that the extent of their 'internality' will be tempered by experience.

To date, research on locus of control of the entrepreneur has yielded conflicting results. If further work is to be carried out using the locus of control concept, multiple measures need to be taken within a stratified sample of business owners. One way forward might be: (a) to collect sufficient background information to examine the possible mediating effects of other variables including adverse experience; (b) to use ratings of key business behaviours which might be expected to be associated with internality or externality and to relate such measures to the locus of control scores; and, (c) to examine these measures in relation to a series of performance outcomes.

Risk-taking

Considerable research has been undertaken in pursuit of the notion that a fundamental characteristic of the entrepreneur is his or her propensity to take risks (McClelland, 1961; Palmer 1971; Kilby, 1971; Brockhaus, 1982). The usual interpretation of a risk-taker is someone who, in the context of a business venture, pursues a business idea when the probability of succeeding is low. Lay or stereotypic notions of the entrepreneur assume that he or she is typically a risk-taker. However, current thinking does not entirely agree with this idea, for Timmons *et al.* (1985) following McClelland (1961) advocate that entrepreneurs take *calculated* risks. Indeed, Carland *et al.* (1984), following Schumpeter (1934), suggest that risk-taking is a characteristic of business ownership and not of entrepreneurship *per se*. The empirical evidence is equivocal in that Hull *et al.* (1980) found potential entrepreneurs to have a greater propensity to take risks. Their definition of 'entrepreneur' included anyone who owned a business, assumed risk for the sake of profit *and* had the explicit intention of expanding the business. Whereas Brockhaus (1980b) defined 'entrepreneur' as an owner-manager of a business venture not employed elsewhere and confined his sample to people who had very recently decided to become owner-managers. He could not distinguish the risk-taking propensity of new entrepreneurs from managers or from the general population. Brockhaus avoided the complication of whether the 'entrepreneurial' venture was a success. He speculated that *established* entrepreneurs might appear to be *more* moderate risk-takers because those entrepreneurs with a propensity towards low or high levels of risk-taking might cease to be entrepreneurs at a greater rate than those with a propensity towards moderate risk-taking.

Other researchers have taken this line of argument further and made a strong connection between success and the degree of risk-taking. It has been argued that, given that some risk of failure must be attached to any business undertaking, then the successful entrepreneur is the one who takes *calculated risks* (Timmons *et al.*, 1985). According to Meredith *et al.* (1982, p.25):

They enjoy the excitement of a challenge, but they don't gamble.

Entrepreneurs avoid low-risk situations because there is a lack of challenge and avoid high-risk situations because they want to succeed. They like achievable challenges.

This interpretation agrees fully with the McClelland and Atkinson research on achievement motivation, where the high achiever has been demonstrated as one who takes medium level (calculated) risks (McClelland, 1961; Atkinson and Birch, 1979). This analysis is consonant with a study conducted by Julian *et al.* (1968) who found that people with an internal locus of control were less likely to engage in risky behaviour than were those with an external locus of control. It would seem to follow from this research that owner-managers who have an internal locus of control will be medium risk-takers, whereas those owner-managers who are externals will tend to take low or high risks. There is evidence to corroborate this view. A study by Miller and Friesen (1982) showed that chief executives with an external locus of control were conservative in their decision-making, whereas chief executives with an internal locus of control were more prepared to adopt 'bold and imaginative' strategies. It was concluded that 'internal' chief executives were more innovative and, consequently, more entrepreneurial.

It might be argued that the propensity to take calculated risks is associated with the strategic behaviour of the entrepreneur. This assertion gains support from the work of Hoy and Carland (1983) who have demonstrated that strategic behaviour differentiates between entrepreneurs and small business owners, whereas, 'selected personal traits [did not hold up] as distinguishing characteristics' (p.164).

What is to be made of such apparently contradictory evidence? A key issue appears to be: from whose perspective is the decision or action considered to be risky? A multiple perspectives approach facilitates clearer thinking. Thus, from an observer's perspective the business person or entrepreneur may be viewed as a risk-taker. That is, in the sense in which risk-taking has been defined, even a decision to do nothing may involve a high risk. From the business person's perspective, he or she may see themselves as 'hedging their bets' and attempting to minimise risk. The adoption of a risk minimisation strategy may be said to rest on: (1) information seeking and awareness; (2) the ability to devise imaginative solutions to problems; and, (3) supreme confidence in the solution and hence the decision. It is in this sense that the entrepreneur might be said to take calculated risks and why it is evident that some entrepreneurs express an aversion to risk-taking (Burns and Kippenberger, 1988).

The trait approach reconsidered

The so called 'crisis' in personality psychology erupted in the 1960s, and a quarter of a century later it has not been resolved entirely but there have been considerable advances in thinking. There have been attempts to improve the validity of trait measures, to redefine traits and to replace the basic personality paradigm (Hettema and Kenrick, 1989).

Empirical attempts to measure particular entrepreneurial traits have yielded conflicting results. However, such work either preceded or appeared to ignore the criticisms which were mounting against the traditional trait approach. On the other hand, such results could be explained by: (a) the invalidity of the trait measure; (b) the supposition that the population to which the measure is applied has not been adequately defined, for instance, different researchers have used different definitions of 'entrepreneur'; (c) insufficient attempts to describe and control for variation in that population. Revisions in thinking in personality psychology have suggested several possible ways forward. These are:

1　More radical ways of conceiving of entrepreneurial traits.
2　The revision of instruments for measuring entrepreneurial traits.
3　The development of instruments to measure situational variables so that the interaction between entrepreneurial traits and pertinent situations can be examined.
4　The development of models of the entrepreneurial process whereby entrepreneurial behaviours exhibited in the business context and performance outcomes can be measured.

THE IDENTIFICATION OF PROFILES OF ENTREPRENEURIAL CHARACTERISTICS

During the 1980s, there have been attempts to derive a constellation of traits which individuate the entrepreneurial personality.

A systematically conducted psychological study has been reported on by McClelland (1987). Research was carried out with McBer & Co. funded by the U.S. Agency for International Development. The purpose of the work was to answer the question whether or not there are key competencies which are needed for *entrepreneurial success*. The researchers distinguished between a group of twelve 'successful entrepreneurs' and twelve 'average entrepreneurs' in each of three types of business (manufacturing, service, marketing or trading) in each of three developing countries (India, Malawi and Ecuador). Their usage of the term 'entrepreneur' would seem to encompass all types of small business owners. They devised a method they called the Behavioural Event Interview (BEI) which appears to be similar to the Critical Incident technique (Flanagan, 1954). The BEI requires the respondent to give an account of critical incidents and episodes in the life of the business. The resultant tape-recorded interviews are transcribed and coded. A group of 'judges' are then required to identify the kinds of competencies revealed. Using this method these researchers were able to identify nine competencies which were significantly more characteristic of successful than of average entrepreneurs. These nine were grouped into three categories – *Proactivity*, *Achievement orientation* and *Commitment to others*.

Proactivity included the characteristics: initiative and assertiveness. Achievement orientation comprised five competencies: the ability to see and act on opportunities, efficiency orientation, concern for high quality work, systematic planning and monitoring. Commitment to others included two competencies: a commitment to the work contract and the recognition of the importance of business relationships. The latter suggests the unusual ability to combine both a task and people orientation.

McClelland also reported on a set of six attributes which were *not* more characteristic of successful than average owner-managers. These attributes were: self-confidence, persistence, persuasion, use of influence strategies, expertise, and information-seeking. Unfortunately this study did not make a comparison with non-entrepreneurs (that is, non-business owners) and it is possible that these six characteristics typify owner-managers in general.

Expert perspectives on entrepreneurial characteristics

It has not been solely the prerogative of the psychologist to identify the characteristics of entrepreneurs. Meredith *et al.* (1982) suggest that there are nineteen traits which may be said to provide a working profile of the entrepreneur. Of these nineteen, they single out six which they suggest are core traits. These are: self-confidence, risk-taking ability, flexibility, a strong need to achieve, and a strong desire to be independent. This list of traits was prepared at a workshop on entrepreneurship. It is not clear exactly how it was compiled and whether it was subsequently tested.

The work of Timmons and his colleagues (Timmons *et al*, 1977, 1985; Timmons, 1989) is one of the most comprehensive approaches to understanding entrepreneurship to date. The models that these researchers have developed would appear to assume that:

1 External factors are influential in shaping the entrepreneurial concern and the ability of the entrepreneur to be successful.
2 The salient characteristics of the entrepreneur are primarily interactive skills (social and cognitive), most of which can be learnt.
3 The entrepreneurial type can be distinguished from other organisational types, such as managers, promoters, inventors, by their personal attributes and behaviours shaped by different role and job demands.
4 'Successful' types may be distinguished from 'unsuccessful' types of entrepreneur.

Throughout their work they have revised their definitions of entrepreneurship in the light of their experience dealing with business owners and the work of other researchers. Timmons (1989) states that:

> Entrepreneurship is the ability to create and build something from practically nothing. It is initiating, doing, achieving, and building an enterprise or organization, rather than just watching, analyzing or describing one. It is the knack for sensing an opportunity where others see chaos, contradiction and confusion. It is the ability to build a 'founding team' to complement your own skills and talents. It is the know-how to find, marshal and control resources (often owned by others) and to make sure you don't run out of money when you need it most. Finally, it is the willingness to take calculated risks, both personal and financial – and then do everything possible to get the odds in your favour.
>
> (Timmons, 1989, p.1)

They claim that the key to successful entrepreneurship is understanding opportunity:

> We do not believe that there is any single set of characteristics that every entrepreneur must have for every venture opportunity. The 'fit' concept argues the opportunity is quite situational and depends on the mix and match of key players and on how

promising and forgiving the opportunity is, given the founder's strengths, advantages, and shortcomings. Significantly, among the hundreds of growth-minded entrepreneurs with whom we have worked, *not one* possessed *all* of the highly desirable characteristics. . . to a high degree. A team might show many of the desired strengths, but even then there is no such thing as a 'perfect entrepreneur', as yet.

(Timmons *et al.*, 1985, p.153)

Of paramount importance to their argument is the premise that entrepreneurial skills and behaviours can be nurtured, developed and acquired and that it is possible to improve an individual's odds of being successful. The younger the founder of a business venture, the higher their energy levels and drive, though the less their business experience, management skills, know-how, wisdom and judgement. They suggest that there are fifteen behaviours which are desirable and learnable. These are:

1 Total commitment, determination, and perseverance.
2 Drive to achieve and grow.
3 Orientation to goals and opportunities. Successful, growth-minded entrepreneurs focus upon opportunities rather than resources, structure or strategy. When they spot an opportunity they let their understanding of it guide these other issues and set goals in its pursuit.
4 Taking initiative and personal responsibility.
5 Persistence in problem-solving.
6 Veridical awareness and a sense of humour. They have a keen awareness of their own and their partners' strengths and weaknesses and of the competitive environment which surrounds them. They have a sense of perspective and are able to laugh, ease tension and get an unfavourable situation back on course.
7 Seeking and using feedback.
8 Internal locus of control.
9 Tolerance of ambiguity, stress and uncertainty.
10 Calculated risk taking and risk sharing.
11 Low need for status and power. The status and power achieved is a consequence not a cause which propels and motivates their actions.
12 Integrity and reliability. It is vital for entrepreneurs to do what they say they are going to do.
13 Decisiveness, urgency and patience. Entrepreneurs must be

able both to make immediate decisions and to take a longer view, sticking patiently to the task until they have realised their goals.

14 Dealing with failure. The entrepreneur must be able to use failure as a learning exercise in order to avoid similar problems in the future.

15 Team builder and hero maker. The successful entrepreneur is not a 'loner'. He or she makes 'heroes' out of the people they attract to the business, giving them responsibility and credit for their accomplishments.

Timmons *et al.* (1985) also identified four other behaviours which they suggest are 'not-so-learnable'. They are:

1 High energy, health and emotional stability.
2 Creativity and innovativeness.
3 High intelligence (that is, 'being street-wise' and having a 'nose for business') and conceptual ability.
4 Vision and capacity to inspire.

Timmons (1989) concurred with the above fifteen behavioural characteristics and suggested that they typify the entrepreneurial mind 'in thought and action' (p.31). Further, he presented a set of eight characteristics which could be attributed to a 'non-entrepreneurial mind'. These are:

1 *Invulnerability*. This feeling is likely to result in unnecessary risk-taking.
2 *Machismo*. This pattern of behaviour goes beyond over-confidence and describes people who try to prove that they are better than others.
3 *Anti-authority*. This exemplifies itself in the rejection of outside help, advice and feedback.
4 *Impulsiveness*. The absence of considered decision-making and the failure to explore the implications of their actions.
5 *Outer-control* (as opposed to an internal locus of control).
6 *Perfectionism* (not to be confused with high standards).
7 *Know-it-all*. The predominant pattern is a failure to recognise what they do not know.
8 *Counter-dependency*. This is an extreme sense of independence in which the individual attempts to accomplish everything on his own.

The motivation of the entrepreneur, as outlined by Timmons and his colleagues, is achievement oriented. An achievement orientation is situation specific: in order for it to be activated at all, there must be an opportunity, perceived goals to be striven for and a desire for a successful outcome. Generally speaking, the situation presents a challenge and a problem to be tackled. Hence, entrepreneurs make an assessment of the likely outcome, know what they are realistically able to achieve and monitor their performance. In order to behave in this way, entrepreneurs must be confident. Only then will they take the initiative and mobilise resources in pursuit of their desired goals.

The entrepreneurial process comprises what the individual brings to the situation and the demands of that situation. Timmons (1989) identifies four principal demands and requirements of being a successful entrepreneur. These are in addition to the more obvious requirements of knowledge and experience of the business environment, team building and creativity. They include:

1 Accommodation to the venture. Entrepreneurs need to be totally committed and give their all to building the business, particularly in the early years.
2 Stress: the cost of accommodation. The need to balance the achievements possible under short-term stress with the ability to relax and ease off when necessary.
3 Economic and professional values. Entrepreneurs must share the key values of the private enterprise system.
4 Ethics. Entrepreneurs need to guard their reputation for integrity and ethical dealing to ensure long-term success.

Finally, Table 3.1 lists the personal attributes and role and job demands of different types of business owner, according to Timmons *et al.* (1977). If such descriptors can be validly applied then, theoretically, it should be possible to identify and measure those characteristics and to differentiate between the types.

SUMMARY AND DISCUSSION

A primary aim of this chapter was to examine critically personality theory and its relevance to research which concerns the entrepreneurial personality. The main purpose of this exposition was to question the idea that it is theoretically sound to attempt to identify traits which characterise the entrepreneur using the *traditional* trait approach. This criticism appears to be substantiated by the conflicting evidence which has accumulated to date, although it is

Table 3.1 Perceptions of characteristics and role demands of entre-preneurial types and managers

	Successful Entrepreneur	Unsuccessful Entrepreneur	Professional Manager	Inventor	Promoter
Personal attributes and characteristics	Personal drive (highly dedicated to business) Persistent Strong character Competitive Independent Takes educated risks Builder Has realistic goals Ethics	Self-centred Unwilling to listen to others Takes big or small risks Unclear goals Money more important than building a business	Proven skills and expertise Can establish goals Can direct and motivate Self-confident Decisive Competitive Thinking about next job Cautious risk-taker	High personal standards Self-confident Conceptual Imaginative Persistent Analytical Loner	Fast-buck artist Short-timer Shotgun approach Ego-motivated Not a builder Gambler Least ethical Super salesman

Role and job demands				
Own values and standards	Same as successful entrepreneur but doesn't meet many of the demands	Oriented to organisation's values, status and rewards	Creative talent	Quick entrance and exit
Hard work		More routine work pattern	Limited business or management skills	Short bursts of activity
Sacrifice		Security builds up	No team skills	Not a builder
Business comes first		Less risky	Works alone	High risk
Knows the business		Management skills crucial	Sacrifice	High return
Team builder		Maintenance and efficiency oriented		Boom-and-bust pattern
Long hours in early years				
Five to ten years to build business				
Innovation and creativity				

Source: Timmons et al., 1977, p.56.

acknowledged that other methodological problems *could* explain such contradictory results.

The problem with such a wholesale attack on the conventional approach to the conception of traits is what to replace it with. One theory which has had many advocates is interactionism. However, this too created methodological difficulties and did not resolve the crucial issue of the concept and measurement of 'traits'. Still, the idea of a social psychological explanation of personality was attractive to the critics of trait theory. And so, in the early 1980s Hampson put forward her theory of the construction of personality. Unlike Mischel's attack on trait theory, the constructivist theory *does* assume that there are consistencies in people's behaviour. On the other hand, in contrast to trait theory, constructivism argues that traits do not reside *within* individuals. They are the result of a social construction melded from three perspectives – the psychologist's, the lay and the self-perspectives. In everyday usage, trait words are used to categorise behaviour as it occurs in context specific situations. There is a tendency for some trait terms to co-occur and thus to be associated within people's minds. Even the trait psychologist, it is argued, makes initial assumptions about the co-occurrence of particular traits when devising personality inventories.

It is clear that when applying trait concepts – personality-descriptive nouns or adjectives – there are various levels of categorisation. The work of Rosch and her colleagues (Rosch *et al.*, 1976) demonstrated social categorisation processes for objects (for example, furniture, table, dining-table, etc.), showing different degrees of specificity for category membership. Cantor and Mischel (1979) adopted such an approach to categorise people using noun phrases. Hampson's idea was slightly different; whilst nouns and noun phrases may be used to develop typologies of people, trait terms are used to categorise behaviours. It is this process of assignation of behaviours to trait categories on the basis of their prototypicality which is of interest.

How can the constructivist approach be applied to research purporting to investigate the entrepreneurial personality? A more detailed account of the methodological implications of Hampson's theory for entrepreneurial research is given in chapter 5. However, it is clear that the use of noun descriptors might be taken to categorise business owners, whilst the observation and rating of behaviours in particular situations may be used as evidence to substantiate particular trait descriptions of the individual.

Not all investigators of entrepreneurial characteristics have concentrated upon single traits and/or used psychometric methods for assessing them. Several attempts have been made to identify the personality characteristics of business owners who are successful. The work of McBer & Co. is of particular interest, especially as non-psychometric measurement was adopted. Lay people were used as judges to distinguish between the successful and the average business owner in a number of communities for purposes of comparison. A biographical technique, termed the 'Behavioural Event Interview', was devised and used to identify nine 'competencies' which were *judged* to be more characteristic of the successful than the average business owners. Although implicit, this work adopted at least two perspectives to account for the personality differences between the successful and the average business owner. It took the business owner's accounts of his or her behaviour over the life of the business and it used independent judges to categorise the behaviour into competencies or personality traits.

Another approach which is noteworthy is that of Timmons and his colleagues. Their perspective on the characteristics of successful entrepreneurs combines the psychologist's and, what we might term, the expert's perspectives. They have taken research on the entrepreneurial personality as one kind of evidence of various entrepreneurial characteristics. They have also used their own experience and judgement over many years of working with entrepreneurs as another kind of evidence to justify profiles of 'traits' which may be said to *describe* the entrepreneur and the non-entrepreneur.

In the next chapter, the entrepreneur is viewed from a number of theoretical positions. These approaches have largely been concerned to view the entrepreneur *in context*. This enables a consideration of the wider, social and business environment, the nature of the business and aspects of the management process in relation to the business owner.

4   The entrepreneur in context

In the previous chapter, trait theory was examined with a view to assessing its appropriateness as a tool for investigating the entrepreneurial personality. Two major problems were revealed. One problem was the equivocal nature of the findings of researchers purporting to measure various traits assumed to be characteristic of entrepreneurs. A further concern was that trait theory itself had been the subject of considerable criticism. In its stead, a social psychological theory of personality was outlined and its implications for research into the characteristics of business owners and in particular, the entrepreneur, was discussed.

In this chapter, a number of other, largely non-psychological, approaches to understanding the nature of the entrepreneur and of entrepreneurship are presented. These theories were selected for scrutiny because they raise issues which need to be examined critically in any book which purports to theorise about the nature of the entrepreneur. They also indicate aspects of business behaviour and the business context which shape entrepreneurial actions. This suggests the importance of seeking to identify particular aspects of the entrepreneur's situation when attempting to distinguish entrepreneurial characteristics and to differentiate the entrepreneur from the business owner. What then are the crucial dimensions of the business context? The concluding section of this chapter provides an answer to this question. However, before that discussion can take place, it is necessary to present a critical review of existing work. This comprises:

1   Consideration of the thesis that the entrepreneur is a deviant or marginal person.
2   An examination of various typologies of the entrepreneur and the entrepreneurial firm.

3 An exploration of the notion that entrepreneurial behaviour is an example of a management style.
4 The conception of behavioural differences in key areas of business activity at different stages in the development of the business.
5 An investigation of contingency approaches to entrepreneurship.

Each of these approaches is examined in turn.

THE ENTREPRENEUR AS A DEVIANT OR MARGINAL PERSON

Kets de Vries (1977) suggested that entrepreneurs are deviant or marginal characters spurred on by adverse experiences in early childhood; they have become 'misfits' – unable to accept the authority of others and to 'fit into' an organisation. His idea was derived from Freudian notions of personality development. As was the case for McClelland (1961) and Levine (1966), socialisation processes in early childhood were singled out as the prime causal factor. The psychological inheritance of the would-be entrepreneur comprises: problems of self-esteem, insecurity, a lack of self-confidence and an inability to accept authority. The result is a person unable to accommodate to organisational life. Their constant feelings of anxiety, distrust and dissatisfaction propel them to search for an occupation through which they can maximise their independence and control over their destiny.

Several criticisms of this theory have been put forward. They are that:

1 There is a lack of empirical evidence in its support (Gibb and Ritchie, 1981, 1982).
2 It does not cover all possible motives for business start-up (Shapero, 1975; Chell and Haworth, 1986).
3 It fails to take into account wider social or societal pressures which might propel individuals into self employment (Dickie-Clark, 1966; Stanworth and Curran, 1973; Scase and Goffee, 1980).
4 The description of deviancy may characterise any number of people in different walks of life. There is no reason to suppose that the universe of entrepreneurs has more deviant characters than any other (Stanworth and Curran, 1976; Chell, 1985).

5   Entrepreneurs are being confused with business owners in general.
6   This type of analysis raises the general point of life cycle effects. By confining itself to childhood experience, it omits the possible influences during the adult stages of development (Levinson, 1978).

Another variant of the marginality thesis is that of the 'displaced person' (Shapero, 1975). Entrepreneurs may be displaced persons in the most literal sense: that is, political refugees who have been seen to produce a surge of company formations in their adopted country. A more common kind of displacement occurs when a person is made redundant or dismissed. Yet another form may be the result of the realisation that they have no future in their present job and have reached a point in life when they must do something about it. Shapero suggests that the forces of displacement are not sufficient in themselves for someone to start a business. Other ingredients which may facilitate this process are an internal locus of control, a role model and possibly membership of an entrepreneurial culture.

Whilst there is evidence to suggest that some entrepreneurs have suffered hardship early in life, or are marginal in the sense that they belong to subcultures – particularly immigrant subcultures – of the population, these characteristics are not universally true of entrepreneurs. Deviant or marginal characters exist in the population generally. Immigrants tend to pursue activities which the local culture allows, this includes taking up jobs which the indigenous population no longer want, in addition to activities such as setting up in business. It would therefore appear that 'marginality' is not a necessary condition for becoming an entrepreneur.

TYPOLOGIES

Smith (1967) focused upon the relationship between the entrepreneur and his company. The idea was to identify different types of business owner and to examine the possibility that the type of firm owned reflected different types of entrepreneur. 'Entrepreneur' was taken to mean any individual who owned and managed a business. The method adopted was to construct 'ideal types' of entrepreneurs and companies. Smith carried out fifty-two detailed interviews with owner-managers of manufacturing firms and from these data distinguished between 'craftsmen entrepreneurs' and 'opportunistic entrepreneurs'.

He found that 'craftsmen' came from blue-collar backgrounds, had a relatively narrow education, a good record as successful workers, and had identified in the past with plant operations rather than top management. As owner-managers they were paternalistic, utilised personal relationships in marketing, restricted their sources of finance to personal savings and money from relatives or friends and followed relatively rigid strategies.

In contrast, his description of 'opportunistic entrepreneurs' was that they had middle-class backgrounds, a broader education, a variety of work experience, and a past identification with management. They are very much market oriented, continually seeking new possibilities and new opportunities. They delegated more, sought many sources of finance, were proactive and developed more innovative and diverse competitive strategies. The firms founded by 'opportunistic entrepreneurs' experienced much higher growth rates than those of the 'craftsmen'.

A recent study by Woo *et al.* (1988) casts doubt on the idea that there are two robust categories of entrepreneur – the craftsman and opportunist. Indeed, Smith's own data suggested that there might have been a third type – the 'inventor'. Further doubt is cast by a study reported by McClelland (1987) who suggests that sociological variables were unable to differentiate between successful and average business owners. Finally, a question might be raised regarding Smith's sampling frame. The very clear dichotomy of class background and type of business owner is slightly incredulous and lacking in predictive value.

Filley and Aldag (1978) used principle component analysis to develop an organisation typology based on three adaptive strategies for dealing with the environment. The organisation types were identified as craft, promotion, and administration types. The nature of the leadership associated with each organisational type was respectively craftsmen, entrepreneur and professional. In general, they found that 'craftsmen' were nonadaptive, inclined to avoid risk, and concentrated on making a comfortable living. Their firms were stable and craft factor scores were negatively correlated with measures of growth. 'Promotion' firms were organised informally to exploit some type of unique competitive advantage. They were centrally controlled by the chief executive and were often short-lived and transitional in nature. They were smaller in size and, for retailers at least, had high rates of growth. Finally, 'administrative' firms were more formalised and professional. They utilised planning, written policies, and budgetary controls. They were larger in size and less dependent on the personal leadership of the chief executive.

Dunkelberg and Cooper (1982) surveyed 1,805 small firm business owner-managers. Using principle component analysis, they produced a classification of three types of business owners:

Type 1   were primarily oriented towards growth and saw their businesses changing rapidly;

Type 2   were oriented towards independence and were strongly driven to avoid working for others;

Type 3   had a craftsman orientation. They were strongly oriented to doing the work they wanted to do and were most comfortable selling or handling technical problems rather than in working on management issues.

In general, business owners classified in this way were found to differ with respect to education, previous functional and supervisory experience, the way in which they became owners, the growth rates of their firms, and the compensation which they enjoyed.

A very obvious problem with such typological studies is that of labelling. The use of the term 'craftsman' to denote a particular type of entrepreneur is especially problematic. This label reflects Smith's original focus upon the manufacturing sector. To pursue a craft has a particular connotation which appears to have been lost with the borrowing of terminology. Further, what of those business owners who are content to make a comfortable living but whose business is far removed from what is understood by a 'craft'? These business owners might be termed 'caretakers' but they do not appear to fit neatly under the label 'craftsman'.

THE MANAGEMENT STYLE APPROACH

Stevenson *et al.* (1985, 1989) reject both the idea of entrepreneurship as an economic function and that it is possible to identify the personal characteristics of entrepreneurs. They argue that 'entrepreneurship is an approach to management' which they define as 'the pursuit of opportunity without regard to resources currently controlled' (Stevenson *et al.*, 1989, p.7). They conceive of a spectrum of business behaviour which ranges from entrepreneurial at one extreme, personified in the form of the 'promoter', and administrative at the other extreme, individuated by the term

Figure 4.1   Entrepreneurial management style (after Stevenson *et al.*, 1989)

	'Promoter'	'Trustee'
	← Entrepreneurial domain →	
		Administrative domain ← →
Strategic orientation	opportunity driven	resource driven
Commitment to opportunity	revolutionary – of short duration	evolutionary – of long duration
Commitment of resources	multi-staged with minimal commitment at each stage	single-staged with complete commitment upon decision
Control of resource	episodic use or rent of required resources	ownership or employment of required resources
Management structure	flat with multiple informal networks	formalised hierarchy
Reward philosophy	value driven, performance based, team oriented	security driven, resource based, promotion oriented

'trustee'. The promoter is the person who feels confident of his or her ability to seize opportunity regardless of the resources under current control whereas the trustee emphasises the efficient use of existing resources (see also Stevenson and Sahlman, 1989, p.104 *et seq.*). They identify six dimensions of business practice by which they elucidate the two contrasting styles of management. These dimensions are: strategic orientation, the commitment to opportunity, the resource commitment process, the concept of control over resources, management structure and compensation policy. Figure 4.1 summarises these two contrasting management styles.

Covin and Slevin (1986, 1988, 1989) have argued, following Stevenson *et al.* (1985), that the measurement of entrepreneurial

Figure 4.2   Organisational structure and management style as they impact upon type of firm (based on Slevin and Covin, 1988)

Management style	Organisation structure	
	Mechanistic	Organic
Entrepreneurial	Pseudo-entrepreneurial firms A	Effective-entrepreneurial firms B
Conservative	Efficient bureaucratic firms C	Unstructured-unadventurous firms D

style of firms will yield more reliable results than attempts to measure the entrepreneurial style of individuals. They define entrepreneurial style as having three dimensions: risk-taking, innovation and proactiveness, and show how it can be related to organisational structure and performance. They distinguish organisational structure according to the Burns and Stalker (1961) concept of an organic versus a mechanistic structure.

> In general, an organic organization is more adaptable, more openly communicating, more consensual, and more loosely controlled. . . the mechanistic organization tends to be much more traditional, more tightly controlled, and more hierarchical in its approach.
>
> (Slevin and Covin, 1988, p.4)

They argue that in organically structured firms, increases in top management's entrepreneurial orientation will positively influence performance, whereas in mechanistically structured firms the reverse will be the case. Such a supposition yields four basic types of firm, two in which the organisational structure and style are congruent (compatible) and two where they are incongruent (see Figure 4.2).

The mix of management style and organisational structure described in Boxes A and D in Figure 4.2 is thought to be incompatible. To be effective, entrepreneurial management style must be matched with an organic organisational structure as signified by Box B. In contrast, a conservative management style is compatible with a mechanistic organisational structure. This yields an efficient bureaucratic firm (Box C).

Covin and Slevin (1988) were able to demonstrate that increases in entrepreneurial activity in organic firms were related to firm performance. Furthermore, the performances of the congruent versus the incongruent firms were significantly different, the congruent firms outperforming the others. They conclude that:

> a strong entrepreneurial orientation . . . is only warranted when other elements in the organizational system provide a supportive context.

> (Covin and Slevin, 1988 p.229)

and that the study indicates the importance of taking a contingency approach to understanding under what conditions entrepreneurial behaviour is most effective (see section, 'Contingency approaches').

THE STAGES MODEL

The problem of identifying those key behavioural patterns which might be associated with different types of business owner has been approached from an entirely different tack by some researchers. This has included the idea that there are behavioural differences in the way owner-managers as distinct from entrepreneurs, manage key areas of business activity. In addition, a longitudinal view of the development of the business has been taken in an attempt to identify discrete stages in that process.

There is no one model of the stages of business development. The number of stages that the business may be said to pass through during the course of its 'life cycle' is highly variable. It can be as few as one (the 'still birth') to as many as eleven or more (Cooper, 1982). The principle focus of attention is upon the types of problems encountered and the consequent behaviour of the business owner (Cooper, 1982; Churchill, 1983; Begley and Boyd, 1986). This lack of consensus regarding a stage model has led some researchers to reject the approach as futile.

Key variables are size and age of the undertaking, given that many of the formal procedures discussed can only realistically be put into practice when the firm reaches a particular size threshold. This should be born in mind when considering the stage models. According to Churchill (1983), Kazanjian (1984) and Flamholtz (1986), there are two aspects to the stages model: (1) necessary changes in the behaviour and management practices of the owner to enable the progression of the business to another stage, and (2) the awareness and ability to deal with the different problems encountered at each of the stages.

Churchill (1983) differentiates between a stage model for business development and for entrepreneurship. Once the business has been founded (or acquired) Churchill suggests there are five stages to its development. These are: Existence, Survival, Success, Take-Off and Resource Mature. At each of these stages there are key problems which typically characterise the business. For example, at the outset the owner-manager is concerned to build up a customer base to ensure viability of the business and to secure sufficient funds to finance the proposed growth. At the Survival stage, the problem has shifted from viability to existing profitably. Once the business is profitable the problem changes in the Success stage to a choice between further expansion or stabilisation. If the latter course is selected, the owner-manager will disengage from day-to-day management and turn *their* energies to other things. If, on the other hand, the owner chooses growth, then the nature of the problems at this stage will reflect that goal and include financing, motivating others and implementing systems for managing growth. The Take-Off stage presents a number of challenges. They include the problem of delegation and decentralisation. Once these problems have been resolved, the business will have reached the Resource Mature stage. Key problems now include the ability to consolidate and control the success and not lose the entrepreneurial spirit.

Flamholtz (1986) put forward a four-stage model of organisational growth. The critical development areas in Stage 1 (New Venture) are identifying a market niche and developing the product or service. Stage 2 (Expansion) is typified by stretched resources. At this stage

> the company needs an infrastructure of operational systems that lets it operate efficiently and effectively on a day-to-day basis. Unfortunately, many entrepreneurs are not interested in such 'organizational plumbing'.
>
> (Flamholtz, 1986, p.35)

Stages 1 and 2 represent the entrepreneurial phase of the company's development. Beyond that, the company must make the transition to a professionally-managed business. Stage 3 is thus the beginning of this process of professionalisation. Typically there is a need for the implementation of formal systems of planning, organisation, development and control.

The fourth stage Flamholtz terms Consolidation. The key area to receive attention is the corporate culture. As the company has grown, the informal systems for the socialisation of waves of new employees become inadequate. To remedy this the company needs to develop a more conscious and formal method of transmitting the organisational culture.

Flamholtz makes a sharp distinction between the entrepreneurial business, which is characterised by informality, a lack of systems and a 'free-spirited nature', and the professionally-managed business. The latter he describes as being more formal, with well-developed management systems and a tendency to be disciplined and profit-oriented in its approach.

Kanzanjian (1984) attempted to identify the strategic and operational problems associated with different stages in the development of new technology-based ventures. His stage model reflects the nature of the business in that Stage 1, termed 'pre-start-up', includes invention and the building of prototypes. Major concerns are securing financial backing and strategic positioning. Stage 2 includes the development of the production technology, acquiring plant, refining the product design, etc. The development of the business in Stage 3 is typified by growth and the attainment of profitability. Sales and marketing predominate. This includes developing market share and providing product support and customer service. Stage 4 is reached when the firm dominates its chosen market niche, is developing a second generation of products and is attempting to achieve a balance between bureaucratic and innovative tasks. The strategic positioning of the business assumes importance once more.

It would seem that any model of the process of entrepreneurship must take into account the stage of development of the business. However, in contrast to the stages of development of living organisms, there is a lack of consensus as to what these stages are and there is no inevitability of progression from one stage to the next: some firms may experience arrested development and these may be run by business owners who do not place growth high on their list of priorities.

CONTINGENCY APPROACHES

There is also the idea of taking a contingency view of entrepreneurship. It assumes that the behaviour associated with the entrepreneurial firm, or of the entrepreneur, is a function of various contextual variables. Some of the more detailed work in this area is that of Miller and Friesen (1982), Miller (1983), and Miller and Toulouse (1986).

Miller and Friesen (1982) chose product innovation as the main criterion of entrepreneurial activity. This enabled them to distinguish between entrepreneurial and conservative firms. Entrepreneurial firms develop a competitive strategy aimed at making dramatic innovations as a matter of routine and take concomitant risks. Conservative firms innovate only when there were felt pressures (from competitors, customers) to do so. The contextual variables selected for distinguishing between the two types of firm were: environment, information processing ability, organisational structure and decision-making processes. In order to understand the relationship between innovation and its context, they suggest that it may be necessary to study managerial motives, ideologies and goals.

The later paper by Miller focused rather more on the behaviour of the owner/entrepreneur, yet at the same time distinguishing between the organisational contexts in which he or she was operating (Miller, 1983). Miller distinguished between three types of firm:

1   Simple firms are small firms which operate in hostile, competitive environments. Their decision-making and entrepreneurial activity are dominated largely by the personality of the owner-manager whose strategic thinking tends to be implicit or vague.
2   Organic firms operate in dynamic and unpredictable environments. Decision processes are decentralised and the personality of the owner-manager is less apparent.
3   Planning firms are more highly differentiated structurally. They tend to be more bureaucratic in their operations and pursue a systematic, orderly process of innovation. Their strategy is explicit and well-integrated in order to be effective.

Miller concluded that:

in Simple firms entrepreneurship is so very tied up with the leader's personality, power and information that *almost nothing else seems to count*. Neither environment, structure, nor decision-making styles seem to correlate with entrepreneurship.

(Miller, 1983, p.783)

Organic firms are much more oriented towards their environment and attempt to develop the best plan from among different courses of action in order to meet and exploit external challenges. The severity of the environment influences strategy and structure, the nature of decision-making and entrepreneurship.

Planning firms tend to buffer themselves from their environment; entrepreneurial activity depends on *internal* initiative. This initiative is a function of their product, their market strategy, and the personality of the leader.

Miller and Toulouse (1986) investigated the notion that chief executive personality is closely related to the strategy and structure of the organisation. The personality dimensions they chose to examine were flexibility, need for achievement and locus of control. They found that smaller firms (employing fewer than 100 people) were low on structural factors and formal planning procedures with a chief executive who demonstrated considerable flexibility. Need for achievement, on the other hand, was found to be correlated with a market differentiation strategy: a proactive and analytical decision-making style and a centralised bureaucratic organisational structure. Internal locus of control was found to be associated with long-term planning and delegation, larger firms and a strategy of product market innovation.

These findings are suggestive of a strong relationship between personality, strategy and structure. A critical research question still to be answered is: under what circumstances do particular characteristics of the chief executive and organisation predominate? For instance, whilst the founding entrepreneur exerts a tremendous personal influence upon the strategy and structure of the firm, mature organisations may look for a leader who can respond effectively to the culture and strategic challenges facing the firm. Indeed, how do such findings relate to the earlier work on innovation? Under what circumstances are owner-managers or chief executives innovative or adaptive?

When looking at firms beyond certain size thresholds, organisational psychologists have regarded the organisation and not the individual as the unit of analysis. Thus a further development in Miller's work is the idea of the *organisational configuration* (Miller and Friesen, 1984). A configuration can be described as a constellation of structuring variables which coalesce to form identifiable organisational types. These include interdependencies amongst organisational structures, production systems, information processing procedures, strategies and environments. They give rise to a small number of extremely common configurations.

An identifiable configuration is that of the entrepreneurial firm which typically, has a simple structure (Mintzberg, 1979); it is small, organic and innovative. The entrepreneur usually retains a tight control: 'its goals are his or her goals, its strategy his or her vision of its place in the world' (Miller and Friesen, 1984, p.77). Two typical examples or archetypes are the 'adaptive firm' and the 'innovator'. The adaptive firm in a moderately challenging environment will adopt an incremental strategy, competing directly on price, product and service offered. In contrast, the innovator cannot compete directly and so pursues a niche strategy; decision-making is typically centralised, organisational structure is simple and undifferentiated and information processing tends to be informal and unsophisticated. The organic way of operating results in informal communication flows, whilst decision-making is typically intuitive; cost-consciousness is not dominant where innovation is concerned. In contrast to this is the 'entrepreneurial conglomerate': the entrepreneurial firm which has pursued a strategy of growth by acquisition. Here the personality of the entrepreneur is said to be critical: he or she is venturesome and ambitious, holds on to the strategy-making power, diligently attempts to identify opportunities, monitors the performance of divisions, and ensures that divisional heads are provided with relevant information to facilitate decision-making.

This kind of analysis is highly seductive, providing a taxonomy of archetypal firms and a parsimonious explanation of their strategic behaviour. What it may enable is the identification of entrepreneurial firms within a broadly-based set of firms and the further differentiation into entrepreneurial types. Further, given the particular nature of each configuration, it follows that the behaviour of the entrepreneur will also differ appropriately. The problem with the Miller approach is that the contingency model tends to assume an entrepreneurial type largely associated with the simple firm structure; Chief Executive Officers are associated with a particular organisational structure and so categorised. There is no sense of progression or of development (except as regards the entrepreneurial conglomerate referred to as an example of an organisational configuration). Further it is assumed that all owner-managing directors of simple and organic firms are entrepreneurs. This confounds the issue when in search of entrepreneurial characteristics.

SUMMARY

People adopt various postures according to the dictates of the circumstances they find themselves in and, as such, their behaviour is usually more readily and more fully understood when account has been taken of this. The five approaches discussed above have focused upon different aspects of the entrepreneur or owner-manager's situation. The psychodynamic approach of Kets de Vries and the sociological approach of Shapero and others have concentrated primarily on the life histories and other developmental influences which have shaped the entrepreneur's behaviour. This has led them to the conclusion that the entrepreneur is basically a deviant or marginal character.

The research into entrepreneurial types is also not without its problems. Prior research does seem to focus upon two dominant types – the 'opportunist' and the 'craftsman' entrepreneur. Key background variables – class, education, work experience – have been selected to explain the behavioural differences in the types. However, the predominance of such variables has been questioned. Further, whilst it is suspected that there are other types, the profiles generated have not consistently converged on a clearly defined category. Again there may be some fundamental problems such as: are researchers using the labels in the same sense? Could there be different types of 'opportunist' and is the craftsman-type really entrepreneurial?

Disillusionment with the idea that there are personality characteristics which distinguish the entrepreneur has led Stevenson and his colleagues to identify six complex behavioural responses which, taken collectively, determine the management style of the business owner. The critical aspects of this are the incumbent's orientation towards opportunities, resources, organizational structure and reward (Stevenson *et al.*, 1989). Variation in management style is conceived of as a continuum ranging from the 'entrepreneurial' at one extreme to the 'administrative' at the other extreme. No attempt is made to subdivide the continuum to suggest the existence of other types. Indeed there is overlap between the entrepreneurial and the administrative domains. Implicit in this approach are a number of personality characteristics, such as 'opportunistic', 'relentless', 'resourceful' and 'confident'. Such a theory could be tested using the Hampsonite model of personality where it is assumed that personality traits are regarded as categorising concepts for labelling behaviours as they manifest themselves in situations.

Slevin and Covin (1988) developed and tested the Stevenson model by relating management style to organisational structure. They were able to show that a mismatch between the two led to a lowering of organisational performance. From this they concluded that entrepreneurial behaviour was dependent upon the consonance and supportiveness of an appropriate organisational system.

Behavioural changes occur as a consequence of the different problems facing the owner at different stages in the development of the business. The identification of such discrete stages is controversial but it does suggest the need for researchers to take seriously the idea of behavioural change over the life course of the individual *and* of the business.

An alternative general approach has sought to understand the relationship between entrepreneurial characteristics (whether defined in terms of personality, background and/or behaviour) and organisational structure and environment. This suggests that it is not possible to understand fully the behaviour of the owner in isolation from business context and environment. The contingency approach is limited by the researcher's ability to identify and measure (in the scientific sense) the key variables and their interactions.

It is clear that the context in which owner-managers carry out their business affairs cannot be ignored if a full understanding of their behaviour is to be gained. The problem is exactly how this might be achieved. In the next chapter an alternative methodology is outlined and in ensuing chapters some evidence presented to illustrate this new approach.

5 Categorisation processes and procedures

It is clear from the preceding chapters that the study of entrepreneurship and the entrepreneurial personality has produced a plethora of approaches which have been defined largely by their discipline base. It is apparent that several fundamental problems of a methodological nature exist. They include a lack of an agreed definition and conceptualisation of the entrepreneur (Kilby, 1971; Aldrich and Zimmer, 1986; Carsrud *et al.*, 1986), the absence of an accepted paradigm (Wortman, 1986) and the inability to build upon earlier research (Sexton, 1987).

Methodological problems such as these have formed the background against which the purpose of our work has been crystallised. The aim is to address the methodological issues rather than to formulate hypotheses such that, ultimately, a set of tools are presented which enable us to accomplish two basic tasks. These are:

1 to differentiate the entrepreneur from other business owners, and
2 to relate types of business owner, stage of development of the business and growth orientation.

This chapter covers three fundamental aspects of the methodology that has been adopted. Firstly, there is a description of the conceptual framework underpinning the typologies of the business owner, stage of development of the business, and growth orientation. Secondly, the method of data collection is outlined. This was principally face-to-face interviews in order to collect biographical data. Thirdly, the modelling of the categorisation process using a neural networks approach is explained.

CONCEPTUAL FRAMEWORK

This methodology is based on the theory of the social construction of personality and the concept of prototypicality, as outlined in

69

chapter 3. Hampson's constructivist theory assumes that traits are based on actual behaviour which is perceived by observers and categorised in trait terms. She suggests the need for a totally different method of personality assessment such as the biographical approach which enables the researcher to concentrate on the individual's behaviour over time. Qualitative data are collected and these may include the individual's own perceptions of themselves and other people's perceptions of them. The biographical approach which we have adopted took both of these perspectives into account.

The task of categorisation requires the identification of those personal characteristics that individuate the entrepreneur. In order to select these characteristics we draw upon the relevant literature and our previous research experience. The process of categorisation has been taken at two different levels:

1 the categorisation of behaviour as being prototypical of a particular trait or characteristic of the individual;
2 the further categorisation of a set of traits as being prototypical of a category of business owner.

When applying this theory to the categorisation of the business owner, a set of key ingredients may be identified such that the blend of these ingredients determines the categorisation of the business owner into four basic level categories. These have been defined in this research study as entrepreneur, quasi-entrepreneur, administrator and caretaker. It is possible to define sub-level categories such as, an entrepreneur who is a 'fast-buck artist' or one who is an 'inventor' type but we have not attempted to achieve such categorisations. In other words, we acknowledge that there are different types of entrepreneur just as there are different types of object such as tables and chairs. We are considering only those ingredients which we think are sufficient to categorise the person at the basic level.

Categorisations such as that of Smith (1967) put forward a typology of the business owner and the firm and sought to examine the relationship between the two. Our investigation did not follow this precise line of enquiry. Rather we sought to define the nature of the firm on the basis of its stage of development and its growth orientation. Stage models of business development have proved to be highly variable, with the number of stages ranging from one to more than eleven (Cooper, 1982). For the purposes of this research three stages were identified: post-start-up, established and professionally-managed. Start-up firms were deliberately excluded. In addition, four categories of growth were identified: declining, plateauing, rejuvenating and expanding.

Subsets of attributes were considered to be associated primarily with a particular typology. However, it is important to be aware of the interactions of all the attributes in determining the categorisations on the three dimensions and that the attributes are not necessarily exclusively associated with a particular dimension.

Type of business owner

A set of defining characteristics of the business owner were identified such that the prototypical 'entrepreneur' and the prototypical 'caretaker' fell at the opposite ends of a spectrum.

The prototypical entrepreneur is alert to business opportunities which will be pursued if thought to have a moderate to high probability of success regardless of resources currently controlled. That is, they will pursue the opportunity in the confidence that the necessary resources will follow. In essence this means that entrepreneurs are proactive, that is, they take the initiative, attempting to control events rather than simply reacting to them.

Entrepreneurs are also highly innovative. This may be manifested by innovation in product or service, markets served, means of production and/or fixed asset investment, which is a modification of Schumpeter's definition. In addition to using available resources, entrepreneurs utilise a variety of sources of finance such as bank loans, overdrafts, hire purchase, leasing and various government or local authority grants (cf. Smith, 1967, pp.46–7).

In developing the business, entrepreneurs strive to be the best, seeking opportunities to enhance the visibility of the company through the development of an image or product concept. In so doing they promote themselves by developing elaborate business networks, thus establishing the reputation of the company and creating a high profile. In this regard the entrepreneur is a high profile image-maker.

Entrepreneurs appear to become bored easily. This results in visible restlessness and a need constantly to modify their environment in order to create stimulation. One other coping behaviour which sustains their interest is the pursuit of a challenge as is demonstrated in many of their business activities. In this regard the entrepreneur may be viewed as both adventurous and an ideasperson. The intuitive way in which the entrepreneur sees an opportunity, and is able to develop ideas for exploiting it, results in a highly dynamic situation. Entrepreneurs thus create situations which result in change. In addition, they see themselves as being adventurous in so far as they are often exploring new terrain. In all these attributes, the entrepreneur contrasts with the prototypical 'caretaker' who possesses none of these.

Between these two extremes we have defined two other categories, the prototypes for which are less clearly defined. The quasi-entrepreneur has many, but not all, of the characteristics in common with the entrepreneur. The prototype is that of someone who is adventurous, an ideas-person, a high profile image-maker, moderately innovative and proactive plus a mixture of other entrepreneurial characteristics. The prototypical administrator is reactive rather than proactive; they are moderately innovative and they may take opportunities, but not regardless of current resources. As in the case of entrepreneurs they utilise a wide variety of sources of finance.

Stage of development of the business

Taking each of the three stages in turn, the prototypical professionally-managed business is relatively formal, of a size sufficient to support a professional management team, and has an owner-manager who has had previous business experience and/or training. The prototypical established business is semi-formal in its management procedures and insufficiently resourced to have a professional management team. The prototypical post-start-up firm has an under-developed infrastructure, low employment levels and has been trading for a relatively short period.

Level of formality is defined by whether or not the company has: (1) formal minuted meetings, (2) clearly defined roles, (3) structured strategic plans, (4) implicit or explicit operational plans.

It is also suggested that there is an association between the age and experience of the person and the stage of development of the business. For example, the younger person with no previous business experience or training is unlikely to be leading a professionally-managed business.

Growth orientation

In the prototypical expanding business the owner is not reluctant to change, intends to grow in terms of people employed, and has demonstrated growth over the past three years by increasing employment and floor space. In contrast, the declining business displays none of these attributes. In the rejuvenating business the owner has shown some reluctance to change but changing circumstances, often brought about by sons or daughters joining the business, result in some actual or desired growth. In the prototypical plateauing business, the owner is reluctant to change and consequently the business has experienced a period of arrested growth, whilst in the short term some contraction may have occurred. However, there is a particularly fuzzy boundary between the rejuvenating and the expanding firm. Rejuvenation suggests expansion after a period of stagnation or decline which begs the question: After how long a period of expansion does a rejuvenating become an expanding firm?

From the above discussion of the categorisation on three dimensions a total of twenty-six attributes have been identified. These are summarised in Table 5.1.

The dynamic nature of the categories

None of the three dimensions defined above is static. For example, the behavioural characteristics of the business owner can change during the life course. In particular, a person who may well have been classified as an entrepreneur in earlier years may be classified as a caretaker in later years as their energy levels, goals and motivations change. On the other hand, it is unlikely that a caretaker type will gain the characteristics that would re-classify them as entrepreneurs. Also, in the normal course of events we would not expect a caretaker to be managing a professionally-managed business. However, should we observe such a situation, we would suggest that this could have arisen through one of two situations: either the business owner has inherited an already professionally-managed firm or the person has 'lapsed' to become a caretaker in later years.

The stage of development of the firm, by definition, changes over time. The post start-up firm, provided it survives the problems and difficulties of the early years, will become an established business. But an established firm cannot regress and become post-start-up. However, there is no guarantee that an established firm will go through the transitional stage to become professionally-managed. This particular transition requires putting in place a professional management team. Indeed, many business owners are unable to cope with the personal changes required (including the degree of delegation needed) and so will cease to develop the business further at this point. This means that the firm can be subject to 'arrested development'. Therefore, knowledge of the age of the business is insufficient to determine its category of stage of development. The speed with which firms can move between the stages can also vary from a very short period for a 'fast track' firm to time periods whose duration spans more than one generation.

The growth orientation dimension is more volatile than the other two as this is subject to external forces such as the prevailing economic climate and the type of industry.

METHOD OF OBTAINING EMPIRICAL DATA

A sample of thirty-one firms was purposively selected to include business owners in each of the four categories we have defined. Twenty-four of these firms were known to us from two previous research projects, one funded by the Economic and Social Research Council and the other by the Nuffield Foundation. Indeed, the experience gained in these two projects has contributed significantly to the methodology discussed in this book. The remaining seven firms were obtained through personal knowledge and contacts within the University of Salford.

Experience of carrying out a number of surveys has led us to believe that, whilst non-sensitive factual ('hard') data are relatively easy to obtain via most methods of data collection, data relating to personal characteristics can only be obtained satisfactorily through face-to-face interviews. Therefore, the data collection was in two stages. Hard data was obtained by means of a structured questionnaire whilst 'soft' data was collected using a biographical approach. The latter was pursued by means of semi-structured interviews which were of approximately three hours' duration. The nature of the interview enabled the research team to focus upon critical incidents in the life history of the respondent and in the development of the business. The business owner was asked to recount those aspects of their personal experience which influenced their subsequent business behaviour, how they dealt with particular problems or incidents and what they felt they had done to enable the firm to reach its present position. Their attention was focused upon particular behaviours and they were encouraged to elaborate by describing these behaviours in context. This enabled the later deduction of personality characteristics. In addition, the interviewee was presented with a list of trait terms and asked to select those which were descriptive of themselves.

The use of a tape recorder was considered but previous experience indicated that some interviewees were inhibited by its use. Instead, the interviews were recorded almost verbatim by means of a secretary taking shorthand notes and the resultant typescripts were subsequently content analysed. The twenty-six attributes were coded yielding profiles of each respondent and their business from which the categorisation on the three dimensions was deduced (see Table 5.1).

All of the business owners interviewed during the course of this study were given assurances of confidentiality. However, five of the thirty-one were asked if they would be prepared to be identified and presented as case studies. They all accepted and their profiles are presented in the next chapter. A selection of the remaining twenty-six is discussed anonymously in chapter 7.

Beyond the profiles and the subsequent categorisation based on judgemental methods, a crucial question is how this qualitative technique of categorisation might be modelled. Recent developments in the cognitive modelling of thought processes present a way forward.

> One way human memory works is by lumping different things together: we see many different kinds of tables each day – large ones, small ones, plastic ones, wooden ones – but we give them all the same name, 'table'. One function of language is to form and manipulate categories. We often do not care about exact details, but whether an event or thing is like other events and things in some useful way. It can be shown experimentally that humans systematically distort stored items in memory in many situations. These are not errors, but are adaptive ways of learning complex environments that display regularities, but where events seldom or never repeat exactly.
>
> (Anderson and Rosenfeld, 1988, p.585)

The unique ability of the human brain to perform such categorisations, as well as problem-solving, learning, remembering and generalising, has inspired researchers to develop systems that are constructed to utilise some of the principles thought to be used by the brain. Artificial neural networks are the result.

Table 5.1   Attributes used for the categorisation of business owners and
their firms

Alert to business opportunities	Yes = 1	No = 0
Pursues opportunities regardless of current resources	Yes = 1	No = 0
Adventurous	Yes = 1	No = 0
Ideas person	Yes = 1	No = 0
Resless/easily bored	Yes = 1	No = 0
High profile image-maker	Yes = 1	No = 0
Proactive	Yes = 1	No = 0
Innovative	High = 3 Medium = 2 Low = 1	
Financial strategy	Broad = 3 Medium = 2 Narrow = 1	
Has formal minuted meetings	Yes = 1	No = 0
Roles are clearly defined	Yes = 1	No = 0
Has structured strategic plans	Yes = 1	No = 0
Planning is informal	Yes = 1	No = 0
Employment	Number employed in 1989	
Age group of owner	55+yr = 4 45–54yr = 3 35–44yr = 2 25–34yr = 1	
Age of business	Number of years	
Has previous business experience/ training	Yes = 1	No = 0
Founded	Yes = 1	No = 0
Bought	Yes = 1	No = 0
Inherited	Yes = 1	No = 0
Has a professional management team	Yes = 1	No = 0
Sons/daughters in the business	Yes = 1	No = 0
Has shown reluctance to change	Yes = 1	No = 0
Wants to grow in numbers employed	Yes = 1	No = 0
Change in employment	Increased = 1 Stable = 0 Decreased = −1	
Change in floorspace	Increased = 1 Stable = 0 Decreased = −1	

ARTIFICIAL NEURAL NETWORKS

Artificial neural networks, or simply 'neural nets', are also referred to as connectionist models or parallel distributed processing models.

In the human brain it is believed that there are at least ten billion neurons, or nerve cells. Each neuron receives inputs from other cells, via synapses, combines them and generates an output which it then sends, via axons, either to other neurons or to organs such as muscles or glands. A single neuron is simple and computational power comes from the fact that they are embedded in an interacting nervous system. Neural net models are composed of many processing elements, or nodes, operating in parallel and connected by links with variable weights. The models are specified by the net topology, node characteristics, and learning rules. Therefore, they are not models of the brain, rather they are models inspired by the brain.

Some of the main characteristics of artificial neural networks are:

- pattern recognition;
- the ability to reconstruct an incomplete pattern;
- the ability to self-organise and learn;
- fault tolerance, i.e. the removal of processing elements from a network will not cause the network to fail;
- the resistance to fuzzy or noisy input.

The analogy between the brain's neuron and the network model's processing element is demonstrated in Figure 5.1.

The processing element is the basic building block of a neural net and has five major parts: inputs ($x_1 \ldots x_n$), weights ($w_1 \ldots w_n$), a combining function ($I = \sum_i w_i x_i$), an activation function ($f(I)$) and the output (y).

A processing element has many *input* paths. Inputs can come from other processing elements, including itself, or sources external to the net. *Weights* determine how much influence an input has on the processing element and hence the amount of influence one element has on another. The inputs and their corresponding weights are combined via the *combining function*, the most common of which is a weighted sum of the inputs. The result is sent to the *activation function* which interprets the result and determines the *element output*. The activation function can be a threshold function which only passes information if the combined input reaches a certain level, or it can be a continuous function.

Neural networks emerge from the joining together of many

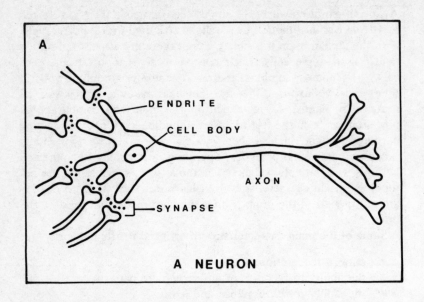

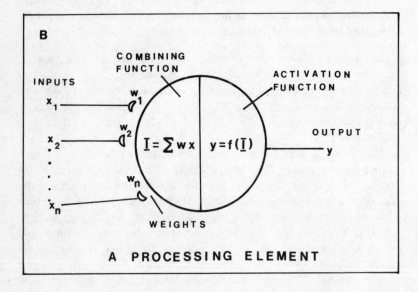

Figure 5.1 Analogy between a neuron (A) and a processing element (B)

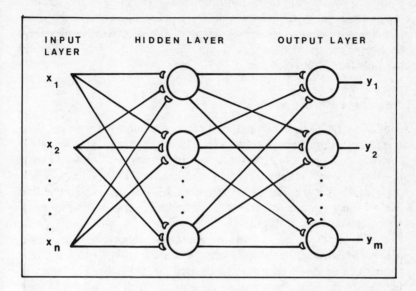

Figure 5.2 A multi-layer network

processing elements. Elements are usually grouped together to form a structure of *layers*. A typical network has three kinds of layer: an input layer, an output layer, and one or more middle or hidden layers (see Figure 5.2). It is important to realise that the input layer does not contain any processing elements; the input nodes merely distribute data to each node of the next layer. For each subsequent layer every processing element within that layer has the same combining and transfer functions and the same learning law. Information moves between, or within, layers of a network and each individual processing element functions independently and in parallel with other processing elements.

As with many other analytical tools, the development of computer power has enabled the construction and use of artificial neural networks based on theoretical models. The subject started to come to the fore in the 1950s following the publication, in 1949, of *The Organization of Behavior* by Donald Hebb. Hebb's work is famous among neural network researchers because it was the first explicit statement of the physiological learning rule for synaptic modification, although the outline of network systems was first discussed by William James as early as 1890. The considerable enthusiasm for neural network research in the 1950s and 1960s was followed by a period of disillusionment and rejection partly because some false and extravagant claims were being made of it at the time. One feature that became important in the resurrection of neural networks in the 1980s was their ability to act as psychological models (see Rumelhardt and McClelland, 1986).

Learning methods and rules

Initially a network is defined with randomly allocated weights. This represents an *untrained* network. Learning, or training, takes place by repeatedly presenting the network with a series of input patterns known as the training set. Then a learning rule, or algorithm, determines how a processing element will change its connection weights in response to experience. The intelligence of the network changes via the learning law.

There are two basic learning methods: supervised and unsupervised learning. In the case of *supervised* learning a training pair consists of an input vector and a desired target vector. The network processes the input to produce an output which is compared with the desired target. The difference constitutes an error which is used to modify the weights and connections in a manner that reduces the error on subsequent training cycles. With *unsupervised* learning no desired output is given. The input vector is applied to the network and the system 'self-organises'. That is, the network develops its own classification rules.

Most learning rules are based on the so-called Hebbian, or correlation learning rule. Hebb (1949) suggested that when two cells are simultaneously excited the strength of the connection between them should be increased. This rule was developed further in the 1950s by Rosenblatt (1959) and Widrow and Hoff (1960) and became known as the Delta rule. It is a supervised learning rule based on reducing the error between the input to a processing element and its desired or target output. The Delta rule is appropriate for two-layer networks but for three or more layers a generalisation of the rule called *error propagation* (or Generalised Delta Rule) is used. The essential characteristic of two-layer networks is that they map input patterns to similar output patterns, but whenever the input and output patterns are very different a network without internal representation (hidden units) will be unable to perform the necessary mapping. If the right connections exist from the input units to a large enough set of hidden units a representation may be found that will perform any mapping from

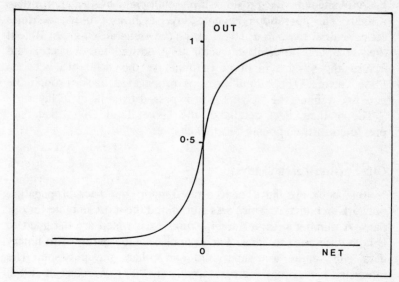

Figure 5.3 A logistic activation function

input to output through these hidden units (Rumelhardt *et al.* 1986, p.319).

Back-propagation and the Generalised Delta Rule

The back-propagation network is currently the most widely used network for supervised learning applications. It is a feedforward network of processing elements which can have any number of layers. No intralayer connections exist, nor any feedback paths from an output layer to a previous layer. Each element produces an output called *Net* representing weighted sums of the previous layer's output. An activation function, usually sigmoidal, converts the *Net* to an *Out* signal, for example, the logistic function, illustrated in Figure 5.3 and defined as:

$$Out = \frac{1}{(1 + e^{-Net})}$$

Each iteration applies an input vector to the first layer, producing a *Net* signal for each element in the layer. This passes through the activation function to yield an *Out* signal that propagates through the weights to the next layer. Each element receives the *Out* of every element in the previous layer multiplied by the appropriate weights. This operation is repeated layer by layer until it produces a set of *Outs* at the output layer. Using the Generalised Delta Rule it then compares the output vector to a desired target vector and adjusts the weights in order to minimise the difference between these vectors. The output error is propagated back through the network training the weights as it is passed from layer to layer.

The mathematical details of the Generalised Delta Rule are presented in the appendix to this chapter.

Other network architectures

In this book we have concentrated upon the back-propagation network architecture which was considered the most suitable for our data. A number of other architectures exist which are designed to handle different problems. For example, some operate with binary data only, some are supervised and others unsupervised. The interested reader may refer to Lippmann (1987), Wasserman (1989) and Aleksander and Morton (1990).

SUMMARY

The purpose of this chapter was to outline the approach used in order to categorise business owners and their firms. The categorisation adopted a judgemental method based on the concept of prototypicality. This was achieved by the identification of a set of twenty-six attributes which were used to develop profiles of owner-managers and their businesses. Data collection utilised both a structured questionnaire and a semi-structured interview schedule. The profiles enabled the categorisation of the person and the business on the three dimensions: type of business owner, stage of development of the business and growth orientation. In developing this three-fold typology, there were several considerations which were taken into account, all of which had to do with time. This temporal aspect was encapsulated in the biographical method, the notion of stage of development, the age of the person and associated life-cycle considerations and the attitude of the respondent to change.

Furthermore, although subsets of the attributes were considered to be associated primarily with a particular dimension, this was not exclusively the case. The interactions of all the attributes also contribute to the determination of the typology.

It was considered further as to how this qualitative technique of categorisation might be modelled and utilised for prediction purposes. The cognitive modelling of thought processes using artificial neural networks was suggested as the way forward.

APPENDIX

The Generalised Delta Rule

The application of the Generalised Delta Rule is in two phases. In the first phase the input is presented and propagated forward through the network to compute the output values o_j for each node. The final output is compared with the target t_j resulting in an error signal, δ_j. In the second phase this error signal is passed back through the network and the appropriate weight changes are made. The two phases are repeated until some convergence criterion is met, such as $(t_j - o_j) < 0.1$ for all j.

In phase one, the *Net* for the jth processing element is given by:

$$Net_j = \sum_i o_i w_{ij} + \theta_j$$

where

o_i is the output from the ith element in the previous layer,
w_{ij} represents the weight from the ith element of the next lower layer to element j in the present layer and
θ_j is a bias similar to a threshold.

The bias is adjusted by the learning process and permits more rapid convergence of the algorithm.

The *Net* is usually converted to an *Out* signal via the logistic activation function:

$$Out = \frac{1}{(1 + e^{-Net})}$$

After computation of the *Out* values for the final layer, the target and output values are compared via the root mean square (RMS) output error:

$$RMS\ error = \sqrt{(E/mn)}$$

E is the error function, defined as:

$$E = \sum_p E_p = \sum_p \sum_j (t_{pj} - o_{pj})^2$$

where

> p ranges over the set of n input patterns in the training set,
> j ranges over the m elements in the output layer,
> t_{pj} is the desired or target output for the jth element in the output layer when the pth pattern has been presented, and
> o_{pj} is the actual output.

The Generalised Delta Rule is a procedure that finds the values of all the weights such that they minimise the RMS output error over the set of training vectors. In the second phase of training, the error signal δ is propagated back through the network and the weights adjusted by an amount proportional to δ. That is,

$$w_{ij}(t + 1) = w_{ij}(t) + \eta \delta_j o_i$$

where η is a parameter which controls the learning rate.
The determination of δ is a recursive process that starts with the output layer

$$\delta_j = (t_j - o_j)f'(Net_j) = (t_j - o_j)o_j(1 - o_j)$$

where

> $f'(Net_j) = o_j(1 - o_j)$, the derivative of the logistic activation function.

To find δ for the hidden layer elements for which there is no specified target

$$\delta_j = f'(Net_j)\Sigma_k(\delta_k w_{kj}) = o_j(1 - o_j)\Sigma_k(\delta_k w_{kj})$$

The derivative $f'(Net_j) = o_j(1 - o_j)$ reaches its maximum when $o_j = 0.5$ and reaches its minimum as o_j approaches zero or one. Therefore, the weights will be changed most for those o_j that are near 0.5 and which are not yet committed to being either 'on' or 'off'. Another feature of the logistic activation function is that it cannot actually reach its extreme values of 0 or 1 (i.e. it is asymptotic at 0 and 1). Therefore, in a practical situation in which the target outputs are binary (0, 1), the system can never actually achieve these results. We typically use the values of 0.1 and 0.9 as the targets even though we may talk of 0 or 1.

Convergence of the algorithm is sometimes faster if a momentum term, α, is added so that having found the δ, the weights are changed according to the following equation:

$$w_{ij}(t + 1) = w_{ij}(t) + \eta \delta_i o_j + \alpha(w_{ij}(t) - w_{ij}(t - 1))$$

The training characteristics of the algorithm may be improved by re-scaling the conventional (0, 1) range of the inputs and outputs. Where the input to a processing element is 0 the corresponding weight will never be modified during training. This can be overcome by re-scaling the input range to (−0.5, 0.5) and modifying the activation function to

$$Out = \frac{1}{(1 + e^{-Net})} - 0.5$$

(see Wasserman, 1989, p.55).

It is quite possible for the training algorithm to find a local minimum of the error function, rather than the desired global minimum, so producing an unacceptable solution. In such cases it is advisable to retrain the network with different initial conditions.

6 Case studies of five business owners and their firms

Many people know or are acquainted with a business owner. They will undoubtedly have views about the nature of the individual's personality and they will probably harbour more general opinions about whether that individual is an entrepreneur. This lay perspective is clearly indicative of an implicit theory of the entrepreneur which, as earlier chapters have shown, has not generally been acknowledged. The key question then is: What characteristics do entrepreneurs have in common?

In the preceding chapter, the terms 'business owner', 'stage of development' and 'growth orientation' were the dimensions which we selected for classification purposes. Key characteristics were identified, which, taken collectively, distinguish entrepreneurs from other business owners. These characteristics are taken to be fundamental, just as flour is a fundamental or basic ingredient of bread.

The purpose of this chapter is to demonstrate the manifestation of such characteristics in five business owners. Other aspects of their personalities are also revealed as is the context, that is the development, of their respective businesses. Indeed, these business owners were purposively selected because they exemplify a number of contrasting features.

1 The sectors represented include: specialist clothing, greetings cards, scientific instruments and industrial estate agency.
2 The ownership status: one sole trader, three limited companies and one public limited company.
3 The levels of family involvement: two are family businesses where the sons have taken key positions in the business (this option is currently not open to the other three). There are two

businesses where the spouse has played a key supporting role at directorial level, and another company where family members have been 'recruited to help out'.
4 The different stages in the business development: all are beyond 'start-up', with three firms having reached the stage of being 'professionally-managed'.
5 The age and experience of the business owner at founding: one business was founded by someone in his early twenties, the others were in their thirties or early forties and had considerable management experience behind them.

In the next section each case study is presented, commencing with a brief description of the nature of the business, its history and development and culminating in an analysis of the key personality characteristics of the business owner. The cases are presented alphabetically commencing with Eileen Bilton, co-founder of the Eileen Bilton Partnership, next Phil Boulton of LIP International, followed by Mike Murray of Cupid plc, then Henri Strzelecki of Henri-Lloyd and last but not least, Don Whitehead of VSW Scientific Instruments. The chapter is concluded with a brief discussion of the categorisation of each of these cases, not only of the owner, but also the stage of development of the business and growth orientation.

EILEEN BILTON OF EILEEN BILTON PARTNERSHIP LTD

Type of business owner: entrepreneur
Stage of business development: established
Growth orientation: plateauing

The Eileen Bilton Partnership was founded in 1988 as a firm of industrial and commercial estate agents, valuers and consultant surveyors. The company employs six people and has an annual turnover of approximately £350,000. Its activity is currently largely confined to North Cheshire.

The company's particular specialisms are the identification of sites, the ability to attract and advise developers and to pre-let before construction is completed. The company is involved in the decision as to what can be put on site, its value, likely return, planning procedures and gathering together a team of people to carry through operations. The team includes architects, engineers, surveyors, marketing people, the developer and the landlord. The company operates through an extensive network of contacts.

Directors

Eileen Bilton (aged 33), co-founder, started in the property world with the Warrington and Runcorn Development Corporation (hereinafter referred to as 'The Corporation') where she worked as the marketing agent for ten years. The Corporation used her name as the first point of contact in its industrial attraction campaign which had national TV and Press coverage. This resulted in many interviews with the press, the occasional radio interview and also opportunities to make television appearances, for example, on the Russell Harty chat show, documentaries and as a member of the panel of judges on ITV's programme Flying Start.

Colin Cawley (aged 37), co-founder, is a chartered surveyor and a graduate in urban land economics. He was formerly Chief Officer (Sales and Developments) at the Warrington and Runcorn Development Corporation, where he had overall responsibility for the disposal of the Corporation's enormous land and property assets. He made many overseas visits and became personally involved with the locational needs of international companies (particularly the USA) seeking property in the Warrington area.

History and development of the company

The Corporation, having attracted 1,000 new companies and 28,000 jobs to the area, was approaching the end of its term and Eileen was considering her future. Having become a household name in the North West of England, Eileen received many offers to perform similar tasks for other organisations but having made a success of the Eileen Bilton campaign she wanted to turn her hand to something new. The only logical way forward was to go it alone and take some of the advice that had been given so frequently over the last ten years.

Eileen knows herself well, her strengths and her weaknesses. She felt she needed a partner to counterbalance what she regarded as her rashness. She sees herself as instinctive and spontaneous with entrepreneurial flair but lacking in some of the technical skills which a partner could, and now does, provide. Both she and Colin knew intuitively that they could make a sound and balanced team.

The business was set up on 1 March 1988. As Eileen acknowledges, it was not a normal start-up situation. The name was known; the company had an existing reputation to live up to and people's expectations were such that her own credibility was at stake. Although it appeared as if they had many enviable advantages as a young company, Eileen believes that a 'cold start' would have in some ways been easier. Nevertheless, they won a major contract from the Corporation which enabled them to set up with ten employees following the planned statutory closure of the Corporation. The contract finished in September 1989. Following this, they secured a number of other major contracts.

At the end of the Corporation's contract the number of people employed in the business dropped temporarily to six whilst Eileen and Colin consolidated their activities ready for the next major expansion scheduled for April 1990. This has been a thoughtful period, considering where they should redirect their energies and thinking through the strategic options open to the company. There have been a number of offers to buy them out but these have been resisted for several reasons, one of which is that the company name is valuable and needs protecting. The company is clearly not standing still and a major expansion is in the offing.

Personal characteristics

Eileen had a grammar school education but left school at 16. Her first job was at the Department of Health and Social Security where she stayed for six years. At 23, she was offered a job at the Warrington and Runcorn Development Corporation, which she confesses was 'by default'. Ironically, the person technically better qualified, who had been offered the job initially, presented herself on the first day only. Eileen was then offered the post in her stead. She worked for the Corporation for ten years as a member of a very successful team.

When she joined the Corporation, the 'property world' was completely new to her. It was a male dominated sector and she preferred to keep a low profile. When she was asked if they could use her name for the advertising campaign she had certain reservations but could see that it presented a good opportunity for the team. Once the campaign started she began to enjoy it, but she steered clear of the media not wishing for personal prominence. Her job was to work with the team to achieve its targets. As the success of the campaign grew she found it more important to detach herself from the name in order to cope with the pressures which were beginning to build up. Apart from being sought after by the media, there were the mildly ridiculous telephone calls which she received; the general public's expectations of her were growing beyond the prescribed role. For example, there was the day a lady telephoned to ask her what she was going to do about the fact that she (the lady concerned) had not received a parcel from the GPO in Warrington!

The Corporation intensively trained their employees and Eileen was no exception. The initial training period lasted for about 18 months before she was allowed to front the campaign. It was a strongly disciplined organization and this self-disciplined, professional approach to her work has clearly been assimilated. One of Eileen's strengths is 'communication' in its broadest sense. She is extremely articulate and able to think on her feet. She can handle her staff, her clients (many of whom are employed by international corporations) and situations where she is expected to speak publicly. Indeed, good communications helps with overall efficiency.

The handling of the human resource aspect of her business is very important to Eileen not simply because the main resource is people. Teamwork she believes is crucial and she and the partnership have consciously chosen those personalities which they believe will be able to coexist and work effectively together. She strongly believes that people should be comfortable and happy at work, that they should behave professionally and with enthusiasm.

At the end of the day, it's all about people, isn't it?

Selecting people to work in such a young firm is an issue she is well aware of. Their expectations should be carefully shaped so that 'they are geared up to come into a new company'. They too must look for business opportunities and respond accordingly. Delegating telephone contact work was difficult for Eileen at first.

It was difficult to believe that anyone could do it as well as yourself let alone better!

It was also one aspect of her role which Eileen thoroughly enjoyed.

Whilst every telephone call is likely to present the company with an opportunity, it cannot afford to pursue them all. Financially there has been no restriction on the pursuit of opportunities; the company is relatively cash rich, funded from its own resources. As things stand at present it would mean recruiting other members of staff in order to pursue what are likely to be one-off opportunities and this clearly would not be cost effective. Major growth plans entail the expansion of in-house expertise. Another limitation is handling the sheer volume of work. Low-level work such as carrying out structural surveys and writing reports is very time consuming. It is important in that it has to be done, but it is not financially very rewarding. Such work is usually passed on to other agents.

The proposed major expansion of the company, which could involve seeking some external funding for the first time, is not perceived as a risk by Eileen. The investment in property has been financially sound (the industrial property market being stable compared with the domestic market) and the critical factor is the timing. Failure has not occurred to her at any point; she is confident in what she can achieve.

Undoubtedly, the Eileen Bilton Partnership is a high profile company. This image is maintained and carefully handled by Eileen. Due to people's high expectations of her and the company, the marketing of the company's image is quite expensive and is constantly being worked upon. The company's logo includes the name in bold navy blue on a white background. Centred above the name is a red cube. This use of primary colours gives a strong image and a clear message. Other publicity material – compliment slips, etc., contain a round stamp with the name of the company which conveys a 'stamp of approval'.

Eileen thrives on change which, given the business she is in, tends to be continual. To keep on developing the business is important from a growth point of view and also to ensure the livelihoods of their employees; their security is important. Eileen is restless in so far as she likes to be kept busy, though relaxed and easeful in manner. She cannot get 'worked up about trivia' and in that respect is easy-going. She is capable of becoming deeply immersed in her work and, even in an open plan office, is unlikely to be distracted. Her courage and strength of character are exemplified by her handling of her sudden rise to prominence and the very public situations she has had to cope with unrehearsed. She finds it difficult to turn away opportunities and rises to challenges with enviable facility. Undoubtedly that sense of achievement and the satisfaction of having tested herself out and accomplished something new is a key ingredient in her continued success.

Eileen is highly organised and believes in the use of business plans, although 'there is a plan in my head which is not quite the same thing'. There is a degree of formality about business operations such as the holding of minuted planning meetings and the preparation of formal budgets. This is, in part, a reflection of the professionalism of the team and the background of its two directors and may be surprising given the company's size. Indeed, the company has moved very quickly through the early stages of growth. At the post-start-up stage the company was still tied strongly to the Corporation. Its first point of transition – the control transition – was disengagement from the Corporation and the establishment of a broader customer base. Having achieved this target the partners find themselves pushing against the resource transition, insufficient breadth of expertise at the top of the organisation to take on certain kinds of work. To have reached this point in under two years is an achievement in itself. Eileen, however, will not speculate about the future. She is quietly confident, optimistic and very resourceful.

PHIL BOULTON OF LIP INTERNATIONAL

Type of business owner: quasi-entrepreneur
Stage of business development: post-start-up
Growth orientation: expanding

The principal activity of LIP is the design and distribution of greetings cards. The company was established in December 1984 in Formby, Merseyside but in 1989 it moved to premises in Manchester. It employs three people on a full-time basis, a network of agents throughout the UK and a number of family 'helpers'. Annual turnover is approximately £150,000.

The customer base comprises independent retail shops, multiples and department stores throughout the UK. The company has also taken the opportunity to sell its product to a Dutch-based company and is extending its overseas markets to Japan and Australia.

Since 1986, Phil Boulton – sole trader – has rented an empty unit within a shopping complex in Manchester. This unit which he has called 'Room with a View' he has made into a retail outlet which enables him to test-market his product and provides him with valuable contacts. The shop itself, possibly because of its location, is currently running at a loss.

Director

Phil Boulton (aged 28), founder, is a professionally qualified photographer and freelance artist. His previous work experience includes two periods of working in the timber trade, first in a sawmill in Norway and later in Sweden.

History and development of the company

Phil founded LIP International when he was 23 years old. He won an award of £1,500 on the 'Into-Business Project' and £1,000 from the Prince's Trust, which together enabled him to start the company. He set up from home with £60 worth of postcards and some photographic equipment. Armed with his 'product' he then travelled to the major cities and walked the streets in search of retailers who would be prepared to buy and sell his cards.

In 1988 the bank gave him his first overdraft facility of £5,000. This was increased to £15,000 in 1989 and enabled him to acquire office space in Manchester and employ someone full-time to carry out administrative duties. In 1990, the facility was reduced to £5,000 due to Phil's lack of collateral – a life insurance policy or a mortgage.

In January 1990, Phil came up against a minor crisis when the office manager unexpectedly left his employ. Following this incident Phil considered a deal with an associate who is a qualified accountant. The intention was that the associate would take over the administration of the business and acquire a 20 per cent shareholding. In addition the company would become registered as a limited company. In a later conversation with Phil it transpired that this option had been abandoned.

Phil began 1990 on a low note. 1989 had not been a particularly good year and he had no reason to believe that things would improve. However, an opportunity arose to extend his product range to T-shirts screen-printed with the contemporary designs featured on his greetings cards. A deal has now been struck with a partner who has his own retail outlet and together they have negotiated a competitive price with a Manchester-based company for the production of T-shirts. By March they had secured orders to the value of £150,000 for the T-shirts, some of which are to be exported.

Phil's export sales appear to have reached a point where they can make a significant contribution to the business. He has now secured orders for cards from companies in Holland, Japan and Australia. He has an order for T-shirts from Germany and is negotiating a deal with a Canadian company. His intention is to increase his export markets to at least 20 per cent of turnover.

Personal characteristics

LIP International is entirely Phil's own creation. At the outset, he had to discover his strengths and then develop them. His ability as an artist and as a photographer, that is, a natural creative ability, emerged. Phil's personal history is slightly unusual in that he is dyslexic – a disability which has tended to marginalise him throughout his life. He did not, for example, do very well at school and his inability to achieve anything, other than the lowest grades on academic subjects, was a problem for him at the time. At the age of 19 he gained some training in the timber trade. His father had been employed in this business for the greater part of his life but Phil did not want to be employed in the family business and he did not persist with it. At the age of 21 he decided to capitalise on what talent he thought he had and went to art college where he completed a two-year course in photography. This was followed by a short period working as a freelance photographer, mostly for magazines.

It would seem that there was a combination of 'push and pull' factors which steered Phil into starting in business. He was unemployed and it was insufficient for him to do nothing with himself and his life. He had, after all, watched his friends go off to university and college. He was left behind seemingly with nothing. He did not resent their success, but his competitiveness resulted in his feeling that he needed to prove himself to himself. He now feels that this period in which he had to think through what he wanted to do with his life has been personally beneficial. He is doing what he wants to do and enjoys his work. In this sense, he sees himself as being successful. This is not to say that there are not times when he feels depressed as his mood can and does change with the performance of the business. Nor does he feel content or self-satisfied. Quite the opposite in fact for he sees the business as a means whereby he can develop himself. As the business reaches new thresholds in its development, more demands are placed on Phil; he has to become more astute in order to get a better deal. However, the 'bottom line' is that the process must be enjoyable.

He feels that he has developed sufficient selling skills that he could sell anything, even toilet brushes, but he would not enjoy it! It is the generation of ideas and the creativity that he takes pleasure in.

From a personal point of view Phil can see the results of his achievements:

> The first three years I didn't have any money. Last January [1988], I had enough money to buy a house. I asked my accountant and he said 'no, not yet'. This year [1989] I invested in the business. Now my lifestyle has changed. I can afford to take people out for meals and this I think of as an achievement.

But Phil will not do things simply for their cash value. For example, he has been offered some part-time teaching in photography. The pay is a pittance compared with what he could earn through his business activities. But he may nevertheless take it up because it will provide an opportunity to make him rethink and reassess his personal progress.

He makes a distinction though between his personal success, as measured by how he feels about himself, and the success of the business. At the year-end, the only way to measure the success of the business is through the value of the turnover and the profit generated. Fundamental to this is the reputation of the business for the quality and uniqueness of its product. But the reputation is also a means to another end: it will bring the desired success which will enable Phil to sell the company and start again, this time pursuing his artistic talents through his photography. It is the pursuit of such a dream that is fundamental to his motivation. This ambition to succeed means that nothing really stands still:

> If you allow stability you are slowing down and then you are not initiating new ideas. You have to be twisting and turning all the time. . .

Phil does not fear failure because he does not believe it to be possible:

> I contemplate what failure could be like but I think failure is losing the momentum to succeed.

Indeed, he is determined not to fail. He thinks ahead, is selective about what he takes on and considers carefully every move he makes. But, as is the case for most small businesses striving to become established, he has to be responsive and take opportunities as they arise which often means making quick decisions.

People say I 'go for it' but I feel I do not pursue them hard enough. I feel I 'blow it'.

Phil has, in fact, let some opportunities for commissioned work slip by, but this was because the work did not meet his personal objectives and values. However, he has extended his contacts and increased his turnover of cards annually. Such opportunities are taken regardless of his lack of resources:

It is a gamble from the printing stage to the selling stage. When you produce you have 120 days to sell it. [I] never really have a lot of money, just gamble it. Sell, get money, produce more, etc. Moved up gradually – £6,000, £10,000, £16,000. But you need to chase the market in the initial stages to allow the gamble to succeed. . .

Phil recognises that in the past year he has made some mistakes. He was unable to sell his stock fast enough and this brought on a cash flow crisis. It is easy to become complacent:

To start shelling out more money on ideas than you should. At the moment I am cutting down because last year I made mistakes. At the beginning of this year I was thinking about survival rather than expanding.

This situation made him think about what to do with any dead stock, offering sale or return, building up even better customer relations.

The temporary loss of his office manager proved to be a valuable learning experience for Phil. He had to become more self-reliant which made him realise how much he could do himself. However, he recognises that for the business to survive in the long term, he needs other people with ability and talent. He relies on a network of people and acknowledges that, like a good football team, the business cannot be wholly dependent on one player.

The chief problem that Phil faces is that of managing and controlling the business. He is out of the office much of the time and needs someone whom he can trust, as he recently discovered, when he hired an individual to man the office and found that he had a drink problem. Phil acknowledges that he does not like administration and that he is very disorganised. A year or so ago he bought a personal computer. A friend set it up for him and left him written instructions so that his office manager could access and use the appropriate software to produce invoices and letters.

The business isn't organised because I am running it. I work long hours and find new ideas and that generates money. I am not practical. I want someone to do a really good administrative job.

There is also the difficulty of using agents for selling purposes – a problem which is not unique to LIP International!

[Someone] sold for me in London . . . I can make more money in one week than he could in one month. He was an agent. He made one sale and then went home instead of pile-driving himself around the shops and then resting. The shops go in waves: they have the money at the same times and run out at the same times. If you do one shop a day you have only covered ten shops in two weeks. You have to get in while the wave is there.

Phil may not be a skilled administrator but he is able to organise the production of new designs for the cards. For this purpose he uses a small network of artists to whom he gives his ideas for a particular theme. They translate them into a design, which they then send to him for inspection. Some designs he will reject and others he will ask to be changed. They are paid through Phil, acting as a middleman, only for the work which is accepted. Phil, on the other hand, is paid for his ability to create concepts; the artist is of secondary importance.

Phil does not like the 'straight jacket' of a business plan although he did acknowledge that the exercise of preparing one did make him think. He vacillates between seeing himself as a business man and as a photographer. He is frequently made offers which are clearly tempting – a contract with a Dutch company is worth £20,000 per year for one month's work. He could take that on and for the remainder of the year pursue his artistic leanings. However, whilst the thought has crossed his mind, he has resisted the temptation.

A deal may be struck with a large customer which can lead to a significant amount of business. Phil no longer has to seek out such opportunities:

They approach me. I have been going for five years. Big companies look for people who can stand the test of time. Some have gone under by now. I keep coming up with new work which is saleable. [These big companies] have better distribution set ups than I could manage on my own. They are laughing at me because I have no expertise to set up my own distribution. But what I have is that I can set up new ideas and be ahead of the trends.

But you are only as good as your next idea:

> When you run out of ideas you are not wanted any more. I work with different concepts so that I always have one to fall back on; always have spare concepts. They will let artists have another 'crack' because of me. Usually when an artist gets one thing wrong they will not use them again. Because I come up with new concepts they are given another chance.

Phil's network of contacts is clearly of critical importance to the success of his business. Most of the artists had started publishing their own cards and Phil made contact with them through 'Room With a View' or they approached him by telephone: 'I said, "Why waste your time selling to small shops when you can sell around the country or internationally?".' Indeed, the size of Phil's business could take a dramatic leap forward. He is considering producing a catalogue, something which he has not done before. He considers that this could generate a further 10–12 per cent more business. Unfortunately, it is not that simple. He estimates that it would cost about £3,500 per year to produce two thousand catalogues to a standard which will meet the expectations of his customers. The product design changes very fast and catalogues will quickly become out of date.

Some things are down to good fortune though: he has tried to hire a much-sought-after stand at the annual trade fair held at the National Exhibition Centre, but so far he has been disappointed. If only he could achieve this, he believes, the business would then really take off and he would have access to fifty different countries. This element of chance manifests itself in other ways. Phil operates instinctively. He feels that he cannot predict how things are going to turn out. In 1989 he thought he was going to have a good year, but it never really took off. At the beginning of the year 1990, he was unsure how things were going to go. But he cannot anticipate the reaction of customers or foresee large orders that might come through. This means that the business is very precarious. His only guide is past sales which he uses as a gauge. Consequently Phil's planning horizons are quite short. As a decision-maker he vacillates a lot – a characteristic which he acknowledges infuriates people. This does not concern him for he is very product conscious. The image he is trying to create is of a contemporary look, of work which is new and fresh. He would like to have a high profile and is pleased if the company is known. His logo, on the reverse side of his greeting cards, is striking.

Whilst he has diversified his product – from posters, to greetings cards and now, T-shirts – the *real* changes are in the ideas that he generates. He operates within a highly uncertain business environment due to the vagaries of fashion for the product themes. He is aware of, and has a healthy respect for, his competitors. Despite the apparent chaos and untidiness of his office, Phil does know what he wants from the business. There are opportunities to be taken which could take Phil nearer the realisation of his dream. He has been in business for six years during which the business has grown and developed, and that in itself is quite an achievement.

MIKE MURRAY OF CUPID PLC

Type of business owner: entrepreneur
Stage of business development: professionally-managed
Growth orientation: expanding

Cupid plc (founded as Cupid Bridal Gowns Ltd in 1980) and its five wholly-owned subsidiaries employ some 188 people and have an annual turnover approaching £5 million. The Group's principal activity is the design, manufacture and marketing of bridalwear with 71 per cent of sales being under their own label (Cupid, San Martin and Jean Elizabeth). Bridalwear design and manufacture is the role of Cupid and its subsidiary Jean Elizabeth. Another subsidiary, Jenny Lynne, producing head-dresses became dormant in 1989 when this activity was taken over by Cupid Accessories Division. A third subsidiary, Bride be Lovely, has four retail outlets, two of which are concessions within department stores. In contrast the fourth subsidiary, Quilty, specialises in the manufacture and marketing of quilted nursery care products. The fifth subsidiary, Brenton, manufactures PVC pram toys and nursery products, such as changing mats and covers for trolleys and buggies.

The customer base comprises some 400 independent retailers in the UK but the four principal bridal customers account for 35 per cent of sales with one accounting for 17 per cent. Exports to the EEC are a recent and increasing activity aided by the opening of a branch office and showroom in Paris in February 1989.

In addition to the manufacture of bridalwear in its Blackburn and Manchester factories, a significant amount is subcontracted. The company's largest source of supply comes from Taiwan. This represented some 53 per cent of its total sales of finished products in 1988/9.

Directors

Richard Lee (aged 45), Chairman, has been a non-executive Director of the Company since June 1987. He is a corporate strategy consultant and a member of the management council of North West Unit Trust.

Mike Murray, F.C.I.S., D.M.S. (aged 41), is founder and Managing Director. Prior to establishing Cupid he spent seventeen years in various administrative and managerial posts. These included accounts, company secretarial functions and industrial relations management with Star Paper Ltd, importing and exporting with Scapa Dryers Ltd and accounts office manager with Henry Livesey Ltd. Selling and marketing experience was gained when he was export manager for Readymade Ltd.

Sue Murray (aged 41), the wife of Mike Murray, has been a Director in most aspects of the business since its foundation.

Alan Wyatt (aged 61), was appointed a Director in February 1989 following the acquisition of Jean Elizabeth and Bride Be Lovely where he had been actively involved since 1966.

Michael Fort, A.C.M.A. (aged 31) joined Cupid as Finance Director in February 1989. Previous managerial and administrative posts were with Thorn, RTZ and DER.

History and development of the company

Mike had always wanted to own his own business and the opportunity arose when his neighbour, who owned three bridalwear shops, said that he was interested in becoming a manufacturer. However, the neighbour was reluctant to take the risk and had no previous business experience in manufacturing. A year later the neighbour mentioned the idea again and Mike, who had complementary skills, listened to his ideas more seriously. The neighbour's strengths were twelve years' experience in the retail sector with a sound knowledge of the product, a ready made customer base and a wife who also had many years' experience of the trade. So Mike, with the support of his wife, Sue, took the plunge and the four of them started Cupid Bridal Gowns Ltd. The company was established in Blackburn in August 1980 with each couple owning one half of the business. Mike and his wife raised the initial capital by selling their house and moving down market.

The partners initially underestimated the working capital required and the potential volume of sales. In 1984, they were over-trading and, as a consequence, they were prepared to relinquish control of a proportion of the equity of the company in order to secure an equity injection of £150,000. This was done to repay loans and to dispense with expensive factoring services, bringing debtor management in-house. At this time the company had a workforce of 32 and a turnover in excess of £326,600 with projections for 1986/7 of a workforce of 105 and a turnover of £1.5 million. However, in August 1984 the neighbour and his wife pulled out of the business selling their shareholding to key management. This coincided with a subscription agreement with North West Unit Trust to provide the sought-after equity injection of £150,000 for a 36 per cent shareholding in the company. These four years had enabled Mike and Sue to acquire a sound knowledge of the product of which they previously had none.

The next five years were a period of rapid growth achieved largely through acquisition. Turnover increased by a factor of 8, from £533,000 in 1985 to £4,354,000 in 1989 and pre-tax profit rose from £20,000 to £441,000 in the same period.

In 1985 the company purchased the assets of Jenny Lynne (London) Ltd, from the liquidator for £30,000 in cash. 'Jenny Lynne' specialised in the manufacture of bridal head-dresses, an operation which was maintained for a further four years by four employees in its original London location. The business has since been subsumed under Cupid (Accessories Division) operating in the North West. This move clearly facilitates the management of the operation.

The next significant step was taken in August 1987 when Mike Murray acquired Quiltessence Ltd from the liquidators. This was a single product, single customer company. The idea was to turn the company round by developing a range of products for the nursery using the basic quilted material. Quiltessence was renamed Quilty Ltd and later resold to Cupid plc in September 1988. The immediate advantage was to provide a counter cyclical product to that of Cupid. This success was underpinned by the significant development of the company's customer base, now standing at around 200.

Permission was granted by the Stock Exchange in September 1988 for shares of Cupid to be traded on the Third Market. The company became Cupid plc and at the same time raised £570,000 via a 'placing' of new shares.

In February 1989 the company acquired the Manchester based retail outlet Bride be Lovely Ltd and the bridal manufacturer Jean Elizabeth Ltd also based in Manchester.

In November 1989 there was a placing of 660,000 new ordinary shares and permission was given to deal in these, together with the existing ordinary shares, on the Unlisted Securities Market.

In January 1990 the company acquired Brenton Ltd in Sale on the outskirts of Manchester.

Personal characteristics

Mike Murray is a man who impresses with his organisational skills and his entrepreneurial flair, his energy and his enthusiasm, and his ability to be constantly bringing about significant changes in the business in such a way as to make it appear almost routine – a matter of course. Mike's route to becoming an entrepreneur was from a sound management background. His experiences as a manager across a range of functions not only supplied him with the mechanics of management, but were also inspirational. In his last post as an employee he had the good fortune to work for the Managing Director of a medium-sized company. This man had stature; he was a charismatic figure who acted as a role model not only for Mike but also for the other senior managers in the team. Mike identified the qualities of this man as being: imagination, a sense of adventure, good housekeeping, pride and self-discipline. To have imagination meant to have a vision of the future, viewing the journey with a spirit of adventure. Good housekeeping suggested things were under control; management were not in a position of being forced to react to circumstances, putting out fires without really knowing how they had started, while to take pride in what was being done and achieved created a sense of well being, of achievement and self-worth. Self-discipline was important to demonstrate self-control, not to indulge oneself and abuse one's position, but also to be able to expect such disciplined behaviour from others – leadership by example not dictat. Such strictures placed demands upon the management team, individually and collectively. As Mike pointed out, 'With Mr X you either quit or stayed to grow stronger and learn'.

What was the evidence to suggest that Mike had assimilated these characteristics? Had he got imagination, for example? He appeared to have a vision of where the business was at its various stages of development. In a business plan compiled in 1984 he mapped out, in considerable detail, where he imagined the business would be, given a certain level of investment. This was supported by forecasts and projections. When we talked to him three years ago his 'dream' of floating the company on the Unlisted Securities Market was already taking shape. There are also other senses in which his imagination has exhibited itself. He purchased Quiltessence from the liquidators and when it started trading as Quilty concerted efforts were made to move away from the one product – quilted seat covering for children's car seats – and to develop the product line into nursery care items. Cupid as a group of companies was beginning to develop a concept; first the bridalwear, then the nursery care. The question is: what other related businesses could Mike develop given this concept? In terms of the nature of the business, he had started in manufacturing and recently gone into the wholesaling and retailing of the product. The next step he imagined was what services could he offer? Needless to say, Mike's imagination has taken the business another step further not only in his imagination, but in actuality as he makes the necessary moves to bring his latest idea into practice.

It is difficult to resist drawing the conclusion on the above evidence alone that the development of Cupid has been an adventure and still continues to be. It is an adventure in which the journey has been enjoyed. Mike immerses himself in the task with total commitment and enthusiasm. That energy and dynamism spill over and motivate his staff, some of whom have been with him since the start. The 'good housekeeping' manifests itself in a number of ways. There is the very obvious sense whereby a clean and bright factory environment creates pleasant working conditions. There is also the careful and organised way in which administration is dealt with. From very early days a personal computer system was installed with software capable of producing management accounts, stock control and ordering. This system has since been updated to include such things as production planning and a network which links all factories to a central computer in order to centralise information. This optimises organisational flexibility and responsiveness in terms of executive action, decision-making and control. Information is produced on a weekly basis, but only that information which is necessary and useful.

Pride is more difficult to assess. There is the fact that the BBC

Panorama team were interviewing Mike for a programme on North West businesses. He was clearly pleased about that. Pride, however is associated with believing in oneself and what one is trying to achieve. This sense of pride is also apparent with Mike. He is assured and confident that what he is doing is right and that other people can learn by his example. Mike communicates easily; he draws on the lessons he has learnt and passes them on. There is a generosity of spirit there which is kindly meant. His self-discipline appears to be quite deep seated, arising perhaps from his working-class upbringing and exemplified in his attitude towards money. He would not, he acknowledged, be content with a steady income to meet his needs and those of his family.

> I want to grow, to be rich. Everyone benefits – the local pub benefits [through bigger tips]. . . [Besides] it's nice to wear good clothes. . . [But money isn't what it's all about] I took a party of customers out for a meal. It cost £250; that made me think about values. . . but you cannot look penny pinching.

Mike agrees that he pursues opportunities relentlessly. As he put it, 'I am too nosey; I like to get involved'. Curiosity then leads to an awareness of opportunities and motivates the necessary follow-through. 'If you are not there you will not see anything. You have to be there.' But this is not all, the scarcity of resources does not deter exploitation of opportunities. When the opportunity to purchase Quilty arose it was through a chance conversation that Mike learnt that the company was going into liquidation. He informed his shareholders, but they were unable to come to a decision and he saw the opportunity slipping away. He remortgaged his house and purchased the company. A year or so later, having turned the company round he sold it to Cupid. This is just one example of his opportunism. He judged it to have been a risk, but an informed and well-judged one. The risks he takes are calculated and backed by the self-confidence that 'you can make anything work if you put your mind to it'!

Mike thrives on change: 'I would knock a wall down to create some interest!' he once declared, rather than let people be bored or become disinterested in what was going on. This is reflected in the very rapid moves he has made in changing and developing the company. His product innovations in terms of design, the development of a range of bridalwear, and the development of quilted products are very obvious examples of innovative activity, but they are followed by a string of other developments, including the investment in specialised vacuum tables at Quilty. These tables have been used to develop a commission cutting service for other garment manufacturers. By his own admission he is 'restless', but one gets the impression that the business is not everything to him, rather it is a means to an end and that end is tied up with the nature and quality of his life. We were surprised to learn, for example, that he can forget about work when off the premises and at leisure. As he put it,

> I can quite easily turn off. You need islands so that you can give 150 per cent hard work knowing there is an island of 50 per cent quiet. You have to be healthy as a leader.

The notion of sound mental, as well as physical, health was clearly important. There were pressures to be coped with; there were times when as a team leader, Mike had to carry others through difficulties.

> We have just had a bad three months. You must not be miserable. Go ask your staff for ideas. We have got a good order book from the shows we've attended. If these orders are not coming through and business is slow the system tells us right away and we can do something about it.
>
> It's important to look after your staff. I paid £1,000 to put an employee back in her council house and then helped her to get a mortgage to buy it. She now pays less for her mortgage than she used to do in corporation rent and I got my thousand back!

Looking after staff might seem, to the cynical, to be self-serving. But this presumably can work both ways. Certainly Mike would agree that he needs people; they are the key to success, he has not, for example, been afraid to delegate, although there hasn't always been someone to delegate to!

> I love to delegate and see people take on new posts. Let them fall down holes in order that they'll learn. Just protect them from the deep holes and let them fall down the small ones.

A key ingredient is the ability to communicate with ordinary folk. Mike tries to empathise and put to them a criticism in a way that he would not object to hearing it put to himself. He says he encourages them to criticise him, but it is not clear how this manifests itself. Certainly Mike is an extremely positive individual in his relations with other people.

Another aspect of employee relations at Cupid was exemplified in Mike's attitude towards growth. Despite the fact that the company has expanded rapidly, particularly in the last five years, there is no sense in which it is 'growth at all costs'. Mike considers that growth has to be carefully managed and controlled.

> It is important in terms of profit. There are two opposing forces: employees have to be safe, but you get lay offs in a weak ship! The company should protect people. If you grow too fast with a rapidly rising number of employees you take a risk. We import, so we can turn off or take less from them. Perhaps all imports should be channelled through manufacturers: we could then compete better.

The development of Cupid plc did not simply happen. Mike went about it in a very purposive and persistent manner. As far as he was concerned the industry that he chose for his business venture did not matter. It so happened that the partners with whom he started up had the product knowledge, particularly in terms of retailing and design. Mike, whose background was predominantly in the paper industry, had no prior knowledge of the clothing industry nor had his wife. The industry is highly competitive and margins are kept low by severe import penetration. Mike's partner was already retailing wedding dresses and so it is difficult to give Mike the credit for having 'chosen' a specialist product line with which to enter the industry. Certainly he took about a year before 'taking the plunge'. From those early years to the present day Mike typically has taken the initiative, been proactive and perhaps somewhat aggressive in his marketing stance. He has not 'let the grass grow under his feet' nor has he let circumstances weigh him down as can happen when operating in a depressed industry. Two things are abundantly clear. They are that he has operated strategically not reactively and that his fierce need to operate independently has been a strong motivating force at critical decision junctures. In the *Annual Report* of Cupid plc for 1989, Mike states:

> The policies which embody the Group's strategy are based on certain beliefs – the belief that specialist niche areas of textile production protect us from the vagaries of fashion; commitment to independence, that is no one product or customer is able to dictate our fortunes; and, lastly, strong professional management.

The extension of Quilty's product range into 'nursery care' was a further application of this niche strategy. The acquisition of two retail outlets has enabled Mike to extend his control over the distribution of his product. His development of a management team through a process of gradual delegation as the company grew and his own administrative strength have produced the strong professional management of which he is proud.

Mike's emphasis on professional management does not mean the development of bureaucratic procedures and increased formality – quite the opposite it would seem. He does not believe in holding formal, minuted planning meetings. Apart from Board meetings, meetings generally are 'a waste of time':

> I walk round and meet people as I go. I think 'roving meetings' are a better description of how I operate.

Indeed, the strategic plan which is written down is constantly at the forefront of his mind, being analysed and modified. He has always operated with a business plan, indeed, in our visit towards the end of 1989, one strategic plan had just expired and another was just about to be written.

> [Planning of that order] needs someone at the head to do a lot of preparatory work. [Ironically] the more alternatives you have and the more cash, the more that can make decision making woolly, if you let it. You have to go back to the original plan and follow it through. . . Things become formalised in your mind. It is important to keep your objectives clear.

The tantalising questions we are left with when thinking about Mike are: What really does motivate him? Is it success which is now spurring him on? The McClelland sense of achievement appears to have been a driving force. He uses profit as a measure of his achievements and likes to have regular feedback. Despite now having achieved so much, the spectre of failure is never far from his mind. Perhaps that more than anything is the current motivator. He feels a greater sense of responsibility towards others than before; he has more to think about and there is more that could go wrong. But Mike is not so proud that he thinks he has all the answers. Neither is he unaware that other people can help him. He has, after all, promoted and rewarded staff who have stayed with him and played an important part in the growth of the company.

HENRI STRZELECKI OF HENRI-LLOYD LTD

Type of business owner: entrepreneur
Stage of business development: professionally-managed
Growth orientation: expanding

In 1990 Henri-Lloyd Ltd reached its twenty-seventh year with a workforce of 300 and an annual turnover of £8.5 million. The principal activity of the company is the manufacture and sale of fashionable waterproof clothing and foul weatherwear for the marine and ocean-racing markets, produced under the Henri-Lloyd label. The company is based at Worsley, Manchester with additional factories at Swinton and Wigan.

The customer base is predominantly overseas, with exports currently representing 80 per cent of sales – an achievement which has had public recognition by the Queen's Award for Export in 1986 and 1987. The name 'Henri-Lloyd' is known worldwide and in Italy it has taken on something of a 'cult image' where some of the garments have become very much a fashion item. This is now spreading across Europe and into Japan and the USA. The company has a presence in the outdoor pursuits' market, but not a major one, and also supplies protective clothing for the Ministry of Defence, the police and other industrial outlets.

Directors

Henri Strzelecki, M.B.E. (aged 64), is Chairman and founder. Prior to establishing Henri-Lloyd he spent sixteen years in various roles in the clothing industry. These ranged from warehouseman, trainee manager with a reputable dress manufacturer, factory manager at a rainwear firm and production director at a company manufacturing protective clothing. He has also been a part-time lecturer at Hollins College, Manchester Polytechnic for ten years.

Paul Strzelecki (aged 36) is Joint Managing Director and son of Henri. He has responsibilities in marketing, sales, and design as well as the general management of the Company. He joined the company in 1978 from Viyella.

Martin Strzelecki (aged 32) is Joint Managing Director and younger son of Henri. He has responsibilities for production, purchasing and warehousing, as well as the general management of the company. He joined the company in 1984 from Levi-Strauss.

Richard Henthorn (aged 42) is Financial Director and Company Secretary. Joined the company in 1974. Responsible for financial and management accounts and general administration including data processing, personnel, and systems development.

Bernard Kelly (aged 58) as Production Director has been in the clothing industry for forty-four years having worked in all design and production departments of clothing manufacture. He has been with Henri-Lloyd since 1976, and was previously employed as Production/Design Director of a company manufacturing men's suits and coats. He is a Fellow of the Clothing and Footwear Institute.

History and development of the company

Henri founded Henri-Lloyd Ltd, in partnership with Angus Lloyd, in September 1963 in a disused chapel and trading commenced in January 1964. The policy was to produce medium to top quality garments and aim for the 'expensive' end of the market. Initially they experienced difficulties largely because the brand name was virtually unknown. At the 1964 London International Boat Show they were able to demonstrate the worth of their product and the company has since gone from strength to strength.

At the commencement of operations, the company had a workforce of six which rapidly increased to twenty employees – the maximum capacity for the site. By 1967 a second factory had been acquired five miles away, employing a further twenty-five people. Two years later Henri obtained additional floorspace in another building where he employed a further twenty people. This growth was relatively rapid, but next was to come a shock which threatened the future of part of the enterprise. The proofing plant which produced their proofed fabric was under threat of closure. Henri made an offer for it and succeeded in buying the necessary machinery and equipment and retaining the experienced workforce. He invited Harold Lindley, one of the top proofing specialists in the UK, to run the company. This change happened so quickly that Henri-Lloyd lost only two days' production. The new arrangement had distinct advantages, which were independence and control over processing and quality of Henri-Lloyd's basic raw material, and proximity to the main factory.

Operating such small units was found to be impractical. The

company could not take on big orders and so it was decided that they should have their first purpose-built factory which was opened in May 1976 and extended to double its size in 1978.

The development of the company was enhanced further as a result of the introduction of fashion clothing, which occurred in the mid-1980s. This posed another problem for the company. Should they subcontract the work or find more space to do it themselves? The solution to this problem was made slightly easier when it became known that a factory in Wigan was about to close down. The factory was in a bad financial position but the workforce of thirty-five was good, experienced and hard working. Henri and his co-directors decided to buy it. This they did in September 1985.

In 1987 a London-based public limited company wanted to buy out Henri-Lloyd. However, the most important asset, in Henri's eyes, is his workforce. Every effort was made to protect this. Had he agreed to the sale, he felt that the factory could have been closed down within twelve months and production transferred to some other part of the world with the consequent loss of jobs. Henri refused to accept the offer and it would appear that his fears were well founded as the London firm was liquidated in 1989. Angus Lloyd, however, wished to sell his entire shareholding. To allow him to do this and to stave off the predatory London plc, the Strzelecki family bought out Angus's shares with the financial backing of County NatWest, which became a new minority shareholder of Henri-Lloyd.

In 1983 turnover was £1.6 million with a workforce of 114 but by 1986 turnover had increased to almost £7 million with a workforce of 239. This rapid growth continued with the number of employees increasing to 300, aided by exchanging the Swinton premises for a new modern and larger factory in 1987, and opening an additional 30,000 sq ft of factory space at Worsley later in 1988.

Administratively the company is well-organised. The company has changed rapidly in its structure over the past decade to allow continued growth in its core business of yachting clothing and its ever-expanding fashion market. A key factor in these changes was the formal appointment of his two sons as Joint Managing Directors in July 1988, allowing Henri to step into the Chairman's role. Today all functional responsibilities are well taken care of, although in the very early days Henri did most jobs himself, including, if necessary the general cleaning of the factory! The company is not bureaucratically run, but roles are clearly defined and there are regular planning meetings involving all levels of management. These include a quarterly meeting of the Board, together with a management consultant, to discuss the strategic issues facing the company. Planning tends to be medium-term and subject to regular monitoring and revision. To facilitate the flow of information within the company, the regular managerial meetings are backed up by talks to the workforce at least three or four times a year. On these occasions the factories are stopped and Henri and the other directors inform the workforce of the state of the company, the market in general, and the main marketing activities planned for the future.

The significant expansion that has taken place over the past five years has been accompanied by the adoption of investment plans over and above the acquisition of the extra factory space. The company has employed more specialised and technical personnel, either by internal promotion and development or external recruitment. All levels of management have been trained to cope with the change and changing environment faced by the company. Additional and up-to-date machinery and equipment has been purchased, including a real-time management information system covering all their operations.

Henri tries to control and plan the pace of the company's growth. Today the company is very aggressive in seeking out and taking advantage of opportunities that occur. However, the company has had to refuse orders at times because management knew that they could not meet them.

Personal characteristics

It takes very little time in the presence of Henri Strzelecki to realise that he is a fun-loving individual who thoroughly enjoys life. He is personable and enjoys teasing and joking with staff and visitors alike. Henri's considerable energy, despite his age, is also striking. Tours around the factory are carried out at a whirlwind pace. Indeed, it is difficult to believe that during the course of a day he can stay in one place for very long! He visits most of the yachting exhibitions, which total 25 per year and, in addition, he gives talks and lectures, mainly on exporting and financial control to institutions such as colleges and trade organisations.

Henri was brought up in Poland. His mother's family were in the road haulage business and his father was a civil servant in the Ministry of Finance. Henri arrived in England as a soldier in August 1946.

He started at the bottom rung of the ladder when he sought a job as a labourer in a British rope factory. He was not offered the job because, although there were advertised vacancies, he was told that they had been filled. The hurt and the sense of outrage at such blatant discrimination was keenly felt. But he had been warned that the trade unions were insisting that certain factories did not employ non-British ex-soldiers. Eventually, at the end of 1947 Henri got a job in the Spencer Wire factory in Wakefield followed by a job at the Wakefield-based Double-Two shirt company. After a few months he had done enough to please the managing director. After a further few months, Henri suggested to the Managing Director that he thought he could 'grow with the company'. At 23 he was told he was 'too old'! Such rejection served to spur him on once again. This time to consider his education.

He applied to the Free Polish Government in London for financial assistance to help with his education. He won a scholarship to Leeds College of Technology and also took courses at the College of Art, the College of Commerce, and Leeds University.

Perversely perhaps, he went back to his previous employer and asked the same managing director, 'What can you offer me now?' He offered him a job as an 'order chaser'. The job effectively was to oversee five clerks working in an office progressing orders. As such he would have no power to get anything done. In addition, another senior member of staff did not like Henri returning with new qualifications. Henri thanked them and looked elsewhere. This took him to another well-known clothing manufacturer (Berketex in Plymouth, Devon) as a trainee manager. The factory had a contract from the Ministry of Defence to supply overcoats. Henri's job was to improve output and quality by achieving increases in efficiency and, if necessary, by replanning the whole department. After three weeks the boss came to see him. Henri told him he knew what should be done but he could not get people to operate his ideas. He wanted to reorganise the factory floor but people would not be moved. He realised that he lacked management skills. He stayed with this firm for six months, during which time his wife became pregnant and wanted to move nearer to her family in the North. He left and took a job as Floor Manager with Alligator Rainwear Manufacturers.

The choice of this job was deliberate. He knew that handling people was his weakness and that the job of Floor Manager would enable him to develop the much needed skills. He held the job for three and a half years before being promoted to Production Manager. The company was facing enormous production and financial problems and the bank gave them six months to turn the company round. Henri was given the job and succeeded in doing it well within the time. He far exceeded anyone's expectations and a promised bonus would have been very attractive had the company not reneged on its offer. After reconsideration a more modest offer was made. It was Christmas 1958, and part of the tradition in the British clothing trade was that Henri, as Manager, should serve the workers their Christmas lunch. At that juncture he was asked if he had paid for his meal, which he had not had time to eat. This was the last straw. He paid them the money and went home in disgust. He never accepted the bonus payment either; he decided that they obviously needed the money more than he did!

Shortly after this incident, he applied for other jobs. He accepted a job as a Factory Manager/Designer for a company producing workwear and protective clothing. The company had a major problem of lack of orders. Henri realised that the patterns for the garments were not right. He altered the designs and where necessary re-shaped the patterns. The situation was still not a happy one. The crunch came when there was a disagreement over an under-costed order which had caused Henri to point out to his new co-directors that it would bankrupt the firm. Henri refused to have his name associated with such a contract and resigned. The company lasted a further ten months.

At the age of 38, Henri felt he had something to prove – perhaps only to himself. He knew that at times he was becoming critical and cantankerous. He felt he could do the job better himself and this was, in part, the cause of the disputes. There was only one way to resolve the matter; that was to set up on his own. He came close to purchasing a factory in south Manchester which produced overalls but the deal fell through.

Henri had designed some patterns for outdoor leisure garments for his previous employer but the other directors at the workwear factory said that their sales representatives could not get any orders. Undeterred Henri took these samples to North Wales whilst on his family holiday. He found that out of three sales visits made, two resulted in the placement of orders for this newly-created yachting clothing.

Henri had a product he knew he could sell and so he joined forces with Angus Lloyd whom he had met some two to three years earlier. They founded Henri-Lloyd Ltd with an initial capital of £3,000, and aimed to produce the best 100 per cent waterproof protective clothing for yachting and industrial uses.

Henri's characteristics of imagination and spirit of adventure are sublimated in the product which has been constantly developed over the years. Henri never intended simply making anoraks or some other type of weatherproof garment. It was a specialised piece of protective clothing which had to be the best. The company now trades on the standards he originally set for waterproof clothing: it is reputed to be the best foul weatherwear you can buy. It took about ten years to establish this reputation. Now Henri-Lloyd's garments are copied and attempts have been made to use an adulterated form of the trade name, for example, in Japan, Henli-Lloyd! Pride in what the company has achieved and in their world-wide renown is of paramount importance. All decisions relating to expansion are taken with the objective of reinforcing that renown.

Henri has taken risks but they have always been calculated. Decisions are often reached after seeking advice, particularly from a network of financial advisers. He acknowledges a degree of cautiousness, but it is not his own security that concerns him.

> No! I am already made. The security of the people here is very important – we employ whole families, mothers, fathers, daughters, sons, who have been, and still are, loyal and hard working.

His ambitions for the company he regards as being not simply for himself but for everyone who works at Henri-Lloyd. They are not about materialism but pride and achievement.

As an individual Henri is a 'character'. He is well-known, well-liked, and respected. Indeed Henri knows everyone in his factories by name. He has been Director of the London International Boat Show, and three other exhibitions, for the past three years and has been voted onto the Board of Directors of National Boat Shows Ltd for another three year term. People invite Henri to give talks which he does with inimitable verve and panache. Henri enjoys communicating what he knows. This is not simply at the 'how to do it' level. Henri transmits, by deed and by word, his philosophy of management practice permeated by his own ethics of business. He has some doubts about unionisation coupled with indecisive management. He believes that good management, communication, morals, and respect for the individual do not necessitate unionisation in his factories.

The company image, encapsulated in its logo is very precious to him. The logo which he designed himself over a quarter of a century ago, is of a gold crown (of the first Polish king, Michael the First) surrounded by a wreath of gold laurel leaves. The name 'Henri-Lloyd' is in gold but he also chose maroon for the remainder of the lettering on the stationery because it too gave a suggestion of royalty and prestige. What Henri-Lloyd produces is intended to be good enough for the most discerning people.

DON WHITEHEAD OF VSW SCIENTIFIC INSTRUMENTS LTD

Type of business owner: entrepreneur
Stage of business development: professionally-managed
Growth orientation: expanding

VSW Scientific Instruments has its headquarters in Old Trafford, Manchester. The principal activity is the design and manufacture of advanced scientific instruments with an annual turnover of approximately £4 million.

The company was awarded the Queen's Award for Exports in 1987 in recognition of the fact that 80 per cent of sales are exported. It has focused upon the specialist research market, predominantly in the public sector. There has been close collaboration with the universities for the identification and development of products. The company caters for the individual needs of scientists and to that end the product is customised from basic units. The company has kept at the forefront of their particular technology by employing a large proportion of graduates and people with doctorates. It currently employs 96 people, nine of whom have doctorates, and also retains the services of eight university consultants. In addition, it funds five CASE Award students.

Directors

Don A. Whitehead, M.B.E., Hon.M.Sc., (age 58 years), is Chairman and founder. Prior to establishing VSW, Don had spent some 28 years in the engineering industry. His particular specialisation is scientific instruments of which he has now gained some 36 years' experience. He served his apprenticeship in a Salford firm and in 1954 he joined Metropolitan-Vickers (later to become AEI) as a draughtsman. Experience in the design and manufacture of scientific instruments was gained whilst working at AEI (Scientific

Apparatus Division) and later as a Director for Vacuum Generators, a company producing mass spectrometers.

Isobel L. Whitehead, (age 56 years), is Company Secretary and wife of Don.

Jon S. Whitehead, A.C.M.A. (age 33 years), is Managing Director and youngest son of Don. He was previously employed as Financial Controller with Fairchilds, California.

Bryan Pemberton, (age 40 years), Works Director, was Don's first employee and has had previous experience as a welder for Vacuum Generators.

Michael R. Brayford, (age 40 years) is Customer Service Director, in charge of the components division. He also was previously employed at Vacuum Generators.

George C. King, Ph.D., is an electron optics expert from the University of Manchester. He designed a range of instruments for VSW in its early days and Don acknowledged his services by making him a director.

Nicholas Long, Ph.D. (age 36 years), is a solid state physicist and Technical Director responsible for specialised electronics and software, particularly for the overseas market. He too has had previous experience at Vacuum Generators.

Brian Hamilton, (age 54 years), in charge of production and purchasing, has had previous experience as Head of Purchasing at AEI.

History and development of the company

In 1976, Don Whitehead started a business in his garage, repairing mass spectrometers. There were just two employees – Don and his wife. In 1977 he registered the company, which had doubled in size, under the name of Vacuum Science Workshop Ltd and moved to a disused mill in Old Trafford, Manchester, where he rented a floor. Further expansion, preceded by a shift in direction to the design and manufacture of advanced scientific instruments, resulted in the renting of more floorspace.

The turning point for the company occurred in 1980 when Don realised that his main markets were not in the UK but abroad. He started by travelling to the USA about six times a year. As a result of this initiative, the company expanded rapidly and by 1985 Don had purchased a building in which to house the business. He also changed its name to VSW Scientific Instruments. Very soon he had taken over the building next door. By 1987, the company was exporting 80 per cent of what they produced and in that year received the Queen's Award for Export. Now the company leases two more factories in the Warrington area. The primary purpose of these units is the development of new products upon which the company's future depends.

Personal characteristics

Don's interest in engineering and things scientific began to emerge during his days at the Royal Technical College, Salford where he attended a course in engineering whilst serving an apprenticeship to a Salford firm (Farmer Norton). In 1954 he joined Metropolitan-Vickers as a draughtsman. It was here that Don's involvement in the design and manufacture of scientific instruments began. During his time at AEI Scientific Apparatus, Don began to realise the potential of university–industry collaboration and to form ideas for the kind of company he would like to own and manage. In the mid-seventies, after spending three years building up a quadrupole mass spectrometry company for Vacuum Generators, he set up his own company to operate as a workshop, designed to establish partnerships between scientific researchers and the technologists responsible for the design and manufacture of advanced scientific instruments.

To Don, the business that he has developed so successfully is rather like a hobby. It has, until relatively recently, involved him working long hours and at weekends. There was a mixture of motives and reasons for setting up the business. These were: the conviction that he could do what his employer was trying to achieve better himself, the intrinsic interest of the work, and the desire to build the best manufacturing company of advanced scientific instruments in the world. The latter motive suggests the need for a challenge – a behaviour for which there was other evidence:

> I have always taken things on and tried to take them to a successful conclusion. When I was 21, I looked at the house market and then decided to build one. Then I had to sell it. It is a challenge. I also had something to prove to those whose business I left.

Don wanted to achieve certain goals and feels that he is still striving to achieve them, but the 'goal posts keep moving'. Now he sees himself attempting to build a successful company with an international reputation, but it was never his objective to make a lot of money. However, Don has not only kept the company in profit, but has succeeded in achieving a level of growth which has ensured a thirty-fold increase in profitability and turnover since the company was founded. The accelerated growth over the past five years was not without its problems. The company was overstretched and 'things were not half done' and so management had to take matters in hand:

> We stopped and spent £300,000 computerising the place. [The result was] the acquisition of CNC machine tools, forty-five personal computers and ten terminals networked to one large computer. This put the business in a position to expand again at a painless, professional rate.

On the other hand, Don has a theory that expansion is easier to manage than a static situation. It is far more invigorating and opportunities are more easily created.

Nothing succeeds like success – people follow a winner.

Don is a complex individual who exhibits a combination of hard-headed realism, respect for scientific achievement, and a determination to succeed. He is not flamboyant, although he considers himself to be extraverted and, whilst he is deeply proud of his company, he readily acknowledges that they have not yet achieved their desired performance levels. He sees his role as a catalyst, bringing the right ingredients together and making things happen. He has developed an extensive network of contacts in this highly specialist field. The network extends abroad from the USA to Japan. He never pretends to be a scientist, but will take scientists abroad with him.

The ability to spot opportunities and exploit them is not on a par with the usual commercial exploitation. It combines a measure of foresight and a willingness to take risks in order to get results. Don categorically denies that he 'gambles on his imagination' rather he gambles on his experience, backed by that of experts. He will first establish the scientific validity of a new idea and then will assess the likely demand by sounding out potential customers.

> I'm a catalyst. I bring people together. I pick out the winners. If a scientist I respect tells me of a new idea I will bounce it off some of my confidants. If it looks promising 'I would invest a million pounds in it'.

The 'picking of winners' does not occur all the time; just the opposite has happened to him on more than one occasion. Indeed, it does not always pay to be 'first in the field'.

Don's view of collaboration has often involved major inputs to research projects at a stage well before a profitable end-product is evident. One scientist has commented that:

> The contribution of the universities to the company has been more than matched by the help that has been given in return. Technical advice and assistance, equipment donated or supplied at cost price, student sponsorship and free fabrication of special systems from parts supplied are just a few of the ways in which VSW has enabled university research projects to get off the ground.

Don is fully aware of the riskiness of the business. The 'wheeler-dealing' and the gambling are all part of the way he operates. Money is not allowed to sit idle; managing the money exchange effectively can mean huge savings or equally huge losses. But one thing he has never done is put the business at risk. He has recognised that the larger the business the more vulnerable it becomes. Whilst the business was small it could get in and out of trouble easily. Now, the business has to be handled more professionally to avoid such risks.

> I used to talk to various guys and thought, 'I will have a go at this', but things change so quickly, you have to have your finger on the button. [They are] risky businesses. We are cushioned with a large order book and a lot of work. A big order book can give you a problem but a nice one. . . [Even so] we have got to see if we can finance new ideas. . .

Don has long recognised the need for good quality staff and team work. He has sought out and employed such higher grade people. It has meant a commensurately high salaries bill! Indeed, at any one time, about a quarter of his staff may be undergoing training, a factor which tends to depress the company's turnover. Communication is important to enable a cross fertilisation of ideas and to raise the level of professionalism. One way in which this is achieved is through internal seminars whereby a member of staff will give a lunchtime talk to his colleagues on the results of a project he has been engaged in. The key is to listen to staff, to be open minded, show you are committed and sincere and to lead by example.

Don has now taken on the role of Chairman and two years ago his youngest son was appointed Managing Director. Don is no longer involved in the day-to-day running of the company nor does he need to concern himself unduly with its financial management as Jon is a qualified accountant. Don claims that he decided to delegate the work when he recognised that he 'was the guy holding the company back'. But he realised this a long time ago. It was crucially important to get talented people in place if the company was going to advance. A lot of self awareness, honesty and self-criticism was needed. As he pointed out,

> I couldn't read a balance sheet but I can sell. Half the business that is coming in is through me selling. That is my forte.

The process of delegation was not easy. It was difficult to let go and Don admits that he was critical of his staff because they were not doing it his way. He suggests that there is a better job being done now, citing the computerisation as an example of this. Don does not hold with formality and 'us and them' attitudes. In the early days, he used to hold meetings in the local pub.

> If we want the old designs we'll have to go in search of the beer mats we used to work them out on!

But this kind of informality he suggests should not be misconstrued as laziness. The work got done and most enjoyably too. Now things have changed as procedures have necessarily become more formal.

There is a toughness about Don's management style: he has been known to 'explode' occasionally and if anyone is found to be 'taking them for a ride' they are told. But he also treats people equally.

> At AEI they had a management car park and an executive loo. everyone who works here is equal – if I come in late I have to hunt for a parking space!

It is blatantly apparent that Don could not have achieved what he has without considerable personal fitness, energy and stamina. There is also a zeal about what he does; a confidence that what he is aiming to achieve is right. Certainly many people have benefited from his achievements. He is not easily satisfied and suggests that the 'day he is, he will probably have to hang up his boots'. Now that the pressure is off him, he is more relaxed, he can do things more leisurely and be two or three times more effective. He has an immense knowledge of the business – a knowledge which has accumulated over his working life.

DISCUSSION AND CONCLUSIONS

It is undoubtedly easier to categorise firms and their owners where there is evidence of a sustained and consistent profile of characteristics which are prototypical. The five firms purposively selected for presentation as case studies demonstrate prototypicality within each of the three categories – business owner, stage of development of the business and growth orientation, with the exception of the Eileen Bilton Partnership. The Partnership is not prototypical of either an 'established' business or of a 'plateauing' firm. The firm is only just two years old and yet commenced with an established name and an unusual degree of formality in its procedures. The plateauing of the firm is in part a consequence of a deliberate policy to allow time to examine the strategic options open to the company.

The business owners of the older firms – Henri-Lloyd, VSW Scientific Instruments and the exceptionally fast-growing firm, Cupid – were easy to classify as entrepreneurs who professionally manage expanding businesses. For instance, all had sought and taken advantage of opportunities and had personally sought footholds abroad in order to promote their products. Henri Strzelecki had one idea for the production of the best foul weatherwear in the world; an idea which he has single-mindedly pursued. Due to the demands of the market place and his design team's expertise, that idea has been developed into a product concept which has resulted in a product range of highly fashionable and much-sought-after clothing. Don Whitehead also had a dream; it was to become the manufacturer of the best scientific instruments in the world. His strategy for achieving this goal was to act as a catalyst and develop other people's ideas for products. Mike Murray knew little about the manufacture of clothing when he went into partnership and founded a bridalwear manufacturing business. His strength has been to develop a product concept and to build a business largely by the acquisition of related businesses. The vision of each of these entrepreneurs found expression in the images they created. Using their network of contacts skilfully, and despite their small beginnings, they quickly created a high profile image, trading on the reputation they were deliberately developing.

These three individuals thrive on change; at the pace at which their businesses have grown nothing has stayed the same for very long. This is exemplified in their restlessness and their inability as individuals to stay in the same place for any length of time. They are people who do not wait for things to happen to them, they initiate change and are highly proactive. Indeed, they appear to thrive on change. In the Schumpeterian sense they are innovators; they have identified product and market niches, and they have used, where appropriate, the latest technology. Their strategies for financing their businesses differ. Mike Murray has chosen to use external sources of finance with the ultimate goal, recently realised, of floating the company on the Unlisted Securities Market. Both Henri Strzelecki and Don Whitehead have funded much of the development of their businesses from internal reserves, although not exclusively so. None of them has allowed finance to become a serious constraint.

The Eileen Bilton Partnership is but two years old, whilst LIP International is six. Both Eileen and Phil have pursued opportunities, although Phil, in particular, has let opportunities go. Phil has travelled throughout the UK initially to develop a customer base and now regularly to sell his product. Eileen has travelled less, her work being largely confined to the Warrington and Runcorn region. However, her involvement in radio and television suggests a type of adventurousness and certainly courage which many people do not have. The Eileen Bilton Partnership is a high profile company, destined, perhaps, to become a nationwide organisation. The image projected is very carefully managed as is the company's growing reputation. Phil Boulton is in the business of creating images, concepts and themes for his greetings cards. The reputation of his business depends largely on his creative ability, the newness and freshness of his latest ideas. Having been in the business for a number of years, LIP International is developing overseas acclaim.

Other characteristics which all five individuals appear to have in common are abundant energy and outgoing personalities. Henri and Eileen are used to public speaking; Henri and Phil have done some teaching, whilst Phil also runs his own football team. Mike and Henri have developed their own philosophy of management which they propound with considerable clarity and verve. Don communicates with expert scientists and is able to use this network of contacts to enable the company to keep at the forefront of its particular technology; he jokes about product designs on beer mats and can look back to the days when communications were that informal. Each has his or her own network of contacts which are used extensively.

To Henri, Mike and Eileen, staff are the most important resource and handling and motivating them well is crucial. Don shares this view, but does not identify his skills as being man-management. Phil does not see himself as a manager and perhaps sees staff as a necessary cost. He recognises, however, that if his aspirations to develop a larger business are to be fulfilled he needs to work with and through others.

As a company the Eileen Bilton Partnership is cash rich. They could grow by attracting key professional management, but they have chosen a much faster route which is to form an association with an established Manchester-based company which can provide the additional professional management expertise they are currently lacking. Phil, in contrast, started his business with very little capital. He recognises his need of other people, but has no wish to grow in numbers employed. He prefers independence and self-reliance. Cupid, Henri-Lloyd and VSW Scientific Instruments are all professionally-managed companies, all three having a chairman, though in the case of Cupid he is not the founder.

The differences in management style and degree of formality of procedures are, in part, a function of the stage of development of the business and also appear to reflect previous business experience. Eileen, having spent ten years with the Warrington and Runcorn Development Corporation, stresses the importance of professional behaviour, of the discipline which work imposes upon the individual and of the need to train and develop staff. Mike similarly has had a professional management background and emphasises the need for good housekeeping, the implementation of systems and procedures for managing the business effectively and the need to arrive at a strategic view of the business. To a greater or lesser extent these key business behaviours are exemplified at Henri-Lloyd and VSW Scientific Instruments. In the latter two cases, however, the transition to the professionally-managed business is more marked. Both Henri and Don have brought their sons into the business, relinquishing their day-to-day control over the management process and assuming the mantle of chairman. Both have adopted the role of extraverted salesman, bringing in the custom, to ensure the continual growth and reputation of the business. Such behaviours were (and still are) their strengths. But, in order that their respective businesses grew further, certain needs were recognised as the next steps in development: to extend the management team, to delegate responsibility and to invest in new technology. Don said he recognised long ago that he was the person holding the company back. Now he can take a two-week trip abroad and on his return discover that things have moved on. In contrast, Phil, with no professional management experience, operates from a rented office in Manchester, with minimal administrative procedures and no formality of operations. With his considerable distaste for office work, and in the absence of a partner with the necessary experience, it seems unlikely that Phil will take his company through the transition into the professional management stage of its development.

The issue of motivation is difficult to tease out. It is complex and whilst there are aspects in common, the pattern of motives varies amongst the five individuals. Certain themes stand out: having something to prove, dissatisfaction with present employer, the enjoyment of a challenge, social marginality, the desire for a change and the recognition of an opportunity. The strongest motive appears to be that each of these individuals reached a point in their lives where they desired a change, they were actively looking for the opportunity, and when it emerged they took it.

In conclusion, this chapter is illustrative of the biographical method of data collection we have adopted. We have taken businesses from a range of industrial sectors, at different stages in their development, and mainly expanding in terms of their growth orientation. Focusing largely on the characteristics of the business owner, we have provided extensive evidence to demonstrate the sense in which the individuals could be viewed as prototypical of the category to which they have been assigned. In the next chapter, the categorisation of a further twenty-six business owners and their businesses is presented together with the results of using a neural network for prediction purposes.

7 Other findings and the application of neural networks

In the preceding chapter detailed case studies were presented in order to give insight into the behaviours underlying crucial dimensions of the personality of the business owners in the context of their businesses. The purpose of this chapter is two-fold: (1) to describe briefly the salient features of a selection of the remaining business owners in order to demonstrate prototypicality and the variation within and between categories; (2) to illustrate how the knowledge gained by the research team, and the methodology adopted, can be used to train a neural network to recognise and predict the category membership of respondents on the basis of their pattern of attributes.

CATEGORISATION

The thirty-one respondents were categorised, on the basis of twenty-six attributes, on three dimensions: type of business owner, stage of development of the business and growth orientation. The prototypicality of the categories within these dimensions was outlined in chapter 5 and formed the basis of the categorisation presented in Table 7.1. The respondents have been referred to by the numerals 1–31 for reasons of confidentiality.

There was no attempt made to sample firms in order to identify prototypical instances for each of the cells of the table. Such an exercise is resource-intensive and beyond the scope of the current work. Indeed not all the respondents and their firms so classified were prototypical and it is the categorisation of these 'fuzzy' cases which also provides interest.

The caretaker

The prototypical caretakers are Respondents 17, 18 and 20. Their profiles are the mirror image of the profile of the prototypical entrepreneur on the person attributes. Indeed, Respondent 17's

Table 7.1 Categorisation of thirty-one business owners and their firms

Type of owner	Stage of business development	Growth orientation			
		Expanding	Rejuvenating	Plateauing	Declining
Entrepreneur	Professionally -managed	1,2,24,30			
	Established			4,11,25, 28,31	
	Post-start-up				
Quasi-entrepreneur	Professionally -managed	7,23,26			
	Established	12	21		
	Post-start-up	3			

Administrator	Professionally-managed	19	13,22	6,14,27	
	Established	10			
	Post-start-up				
Caretaker	Professionally-managed		15,16		
	Established		5,29	8,20	
	Post-start-up			9,18	17

Case study respondents are:

1 – Henri Strzelecki of Henri-Lloyd Ltd
2 – Mike Murray of Cupid plc
3 – Phil Boulton of LIP International
25 – Eileen Bilton of Eileen Bilton Partnership Ltd
30 – Don Whitehead of VSW Scientific Instruments Ltd

growth orientation is also the mirror image of that of entrepreneurs Henri Strzelecki (1), Mike Murray (2) and Don Whitehead (30). He inherited a business which is in a labour-intensive, contracting industry. He serves a mass market with an undifferentiated product. This owner-manager was the only one who did not adopt a niche strategy. Planning was at a level of informality inappropriate for the size of the business which was comparable to that of Cupid plc. Indeed, the management style was often frenetic: that of reacting to problems and 'fire-fighting' rather than anticipating problems and considering how to deal with them. The Managing Director had not developed a cohesive management team to cover the key functional areas. Proportionately, too much time was spent dealing with the day-to-day operational issues and consequently too little time on the strategic. The personality characteristics of the caretaker, when they manifest themselves in key business behaviours, would appear to be fatal for a company operating in a hostile, highly competitive market. It is perhaps no surprise that this was a company in decline.

Respondents 8 and 9 were prototypical caretakers with the exception that they considered themselves as 'ideas people'. In both these cases, new technology products were being manufactured. This was in response to problems which required bespoke solutions that necessitated a degree of creativity on the part of the business owner. Both firms employed less than ten people and, in the case of Respondent 8, there was no desire to grow any larger in terms of numbers employed. The latter company was a profitable concern and the Managing Director could secure enough business to maintain it at that level. This contrasted somewhat with the situation of Respondent 9, where it was recognised that there was an inescapable need to make some fundamental changes in order to secure the future of the firm.

The businesses managed by Respondents 5 and 29 are old-established businesses which have been inherited. Both are relatively small companies (employing fewer than thirty individuals) which in recent years have developed a positive growth profile. Such growth was undertaken with reluctance and in the case of Respondent 5, two major changes undertaken were largely 'forced' upon him.

Not all the businesses with caretaker owners were small. Respondent 16 had a labour force of about 200, whereas Respondent 15 had a labour force of almost double that size. Respondent 15, now Chairman, had founded the business over forty years ago and his son had taken over the role of Managing Director.

Still the Chairman had an influence over the decisions taken. His personality profile was identical to that of Respondent 16: both acknowledged a reluctance to change; the moderate degree of innovation shown was partly a consequence of situational pressures, whilst their attitude to financing the business was narrow and unimaginative. In the case of Respondent 15, it is difficult to believe that the founder of a relatively successful business could have the characteristics of a 'caretaker'. It was clear when he recounted his business activities of the past that he had behaved entrepreneurially, having pursued and successfully exploited opportunities and having been innovative in the Schumperterian sense. However, it is known that some entrepreneurs do lose their entrepreneurial characteristics at a later stage in their lives. The actual reasons for such reversion are largely surmise. It is possible that such founders have developed the business to a particular size threshold and by so doing have achieved their goals. Their motivation then changes to that of the maintenance of existing structures and procedures. This, combined with an inability to let go, may result in manifestations of stubbornness or belligerence, as the founder opposes change as a means of hanging on to the last vestiges of control. There was some evidence to substantiate such an explanation in the case of Respondent 15; there had already been a succession problem in the company, the outcome of which had resulted in the younger son taking on the mantle of Managing Director and the elder son leaving his father's employ.

The situation for Respondent 16 was very different. He had married into this particular old-established, family business many years ago and had been made Managing Director of one of the companies in the group. The company had been badly affected by the recession of the early 1980s and had had to shed labour. This experience appeared to have been traumatic as major changes were forced on senior management in order for the business to survive. A problem for the Managing Director was that of adjusting to the new way of doing things and letting go of years of tradition which had been associated with comfort and security. The challenges facing the business suggested the need for someone at the helm with the entrepreneurial profile identified by this research. The mismatch between the personal attributes of the Managing Director and organisational requirements was readily apparent. Even his effectiveness as a manager was being affected by the conditions created by the less certain, unstable environment into which the company had been plunged. The presence of a professional management team and the implementation of a structured strategic plan, a requirement imposed by an external financier, enabled the firm to work towards the necessary process of rejuvenation.

The administrator

Turning attention from the caretaker business owner to the administrator, it is clear from Table 7.1 that the majority were heading up professionally-managed businesses. Whilst such an association might be expected on the grounds of compatibility between their preferred management style and greater formality of organisational procedures, its predominance might simply be an artefact of the sampling frame which was biased towards older, established businesses.

Respondent 27 was a prototypical administrator. As such he tended to react to circumstances rather than take the initiative; unlike the typical caretaker he was not reluctant to change; he would pursue opportunities but not without regard for the resources currently controlled; and his investment decisions showed that he utilised a wide variety of sources of finance. Respondent 27 had reached that stage of life when, in a matter of only a few years, he would have to face up to the problem of succession. He already knew that his son did not want to join him in managing the business and so it was rather a question of when and how it might eventually be sold. The business had been moving along its usual lines for some time until the directors received the results of a management consultant's report. This suggested that, given the business they were in, they were ideally placed either to acquire a business in France in order to position the company for the lowering of trade barriers in 1992, or to attract a buyer from companies on the Continent wishing to make a similar foothold in Britain. The report advocated the need for a business plan if the company was going to achieve either of these options. Such an intervention appeared to have stimulated the Managing Director into thinking more deeply about the strategic issues to be considered.

The situation of Respondent 13 is entirely different from that of the business owner just described. This respondent bought an established business which relied heavily on a single customer. The traditional buying pattern in this sector had been that of bulk purchases. This enabled the manufacturer to realise economies through long runs and so to plan production to meet these large orders. A change in this buying pattern brought about, in part, by changes in technology has resulted in the customer placing smaller orders more frequently thus putting the onus of stock-carrying on the shoulders of the manufacturer. This change created problems for the Managing Director in so far as his business was geared to long production runs, resulting in low costs and efficiency. He was now being forced to *react* to a changed situation which, due to the size and purchasing power of his major customer, he could do very little to stem. His son entered the company at about this time and between them they set up a separate business unit with new plant, on a greenfield site. The product was highly specialised and would occupy a market niche not yet exploited. The Managing Director acknowledged that such an entrepreneurial venture scared him, it was not his style. But the combination of circumstances – the threat to his existing business, the 'enterprise culture' which encouraged entrepreneurial activity of the kind proposed, and the fact that his son was in a position to manage the new venture – had tipped the scales in favour of going ahead. Unlike Respondent 16, he had anticipated the future problems for his business and reacted to them *before* any damage (in terms of loss of jobs) had been experienced. He was also prepared to take the opportunity before him and persist with it, and in this, and other spheres of his business activity (for example, investment in new technology), he showed far-sightedness, not a reluctance to change.

The quasi-entrepreneur

Distinguishing between the entrepreneurs and the quasi-entre-preneurs in the sample was not an easy task, particularly when judging the non-prototypical cases. The quasi-entrepreneurs tend to be less opportunistic and show less evidence of restlessness. Typically they are proactive and innovative. In this regard they are quite capable of generating ideas and enjoy bringing about change.

Respondent 23 was one of the younger managing directors in the sample, being under 35 years in age. He also possessed another rare characteristic in that he was a graduate. He had inherited the family business and was the grandson of the founder. The company is small (employing fewer than fifty people) and yet exhibits most of the attributes of a professionally-managed business. Indeed, it appeared to be a particular strength and interest of this owner to set up an infrastructure within the company to facilitate its expansion. To this end, he had introduced computerised systems for office administration and on the technical side of the business, and had also adopted the British quality standard, BS5750. His aim was to introduce appropriate systems which would save time and improve efficiency. He was also developing his management team and had introduced a number of changes since he took over from his father. He felt that 'he would soon get bored if things didn't change'. Although he had worked in various departments of the firm before becoming Managing Director, he did not have the technical knowledge underpinning the product base of the company. Consequently, he relied on his ability to generate ideas through his managers. The only product change he had introduced was computerised colour matching which would improve the quality and consistency of the product. However, he had used a consultant to enable them to identify market niches for their product which was unbranded with a very small market share. This respondent appeared to be content with a low profile. He had a narrowly based financial strategy, funding expansion through the company's own reserves. As such, opportunities were pursued with existing resources in mind.

In contrast Respondent 7, who is approaching the age of retirement, is the Managing Director of a company which is more than three times the size of that just described. Here the necessity of introducing formal systems and procedures to manage the business was readily apparent. Indeed, his management ability in developing and implementing an organisational structure, which enabled the integration of a variety of technical skills, has contributed to the company's success. The company's growth was initially constrained by the very cautious nature of his two partners whom he bought out on their retirement. Since then the respondent has been highly innovative, buying up local competition and integrating those businesses into his own. The employment level has increased four-fold over the past five years and is continuing to grow. The Managing Director aired the opinion that the accountants that they had dealt with over the years were probably too small to deal with the complexities of financing the next stage in the development of the business and, as a consequence, the firm might miss opportunities. He himself lacked any financial training and tended to use a 'rule of thumb' approach basing his judgement on what he thought they could afford to spend. A new product had been developed which was thought to have high sales potential but no effort had been made to research the market and advertise the product. Such behaviours demonstrate a certain reluctance to persist in the pursuit of all opportunities. A possible explanation for this behaviour is that, unlike Respondent 15 who is still involved in the business well after normal retirement age, Respondent 7 is nearing retirement with no relatives to succeed him in the business. He demonstrated an inner conflict between wanting to take life easy in anticipation of retirement and continuing to expend a considerable amount of energy in order to develop the business further.

The entrepreneur

Table 7.1 shows two groups of entrepreneur: within one group the type of business being managed is expanding and is professionally-managed; for the other group the business is established and plateauing. Three of the entrepreneurs grouped in the former category have been described in detail in chapter 6, the bulk of the ensuing description will focus upon the entrepreneurs in the latter category.

The first question which arises is: If the businesses in the second entrepreneurial group are at a different stage of development is that largely a function of the age of the business? It is the case that the average age of the professionally-managed businesses is approximately 20 years, whilst the average age of the established group is just over 5 years. On the face of it there would appear to be a positive correlation between stage of development and age. However, to leave the matter there would be to simplify the situation to the point of being misleading. A comparison between the profiles of Respondents 4 and 2 (Cupid plc) illustrates the point.

The age of these two businesses is identical (9 years) and the age of the individuals concerned is also very close (about 40 years). Both businesses are in manufacturing and the *person* profiles of the two respondents are identical. Why then is Respondent 4 not running a professionally-managed, expanding business also? Unlike Mike Murray, this entrepreneur came from a family who were themselves in business and Respondent 4 spent his early years of employment working in the family business. Mike Murray, it will be recalled, spent his early years as an employee and a manager. The key problem for Respondent 4 is managing the transition to a professionally-managed business. Although both entrepreneurs have a business plan, day-to-day planning for Respondent 4 is still at an informal level. Indeed, such operational planning is largely in this entrepreneur's head, the consequence of which is poor communication and inadequate task and role definition in key areas. There is no professional management team. There is one other director who manages production, personnel issues, including health and safety, and who has had the major task of organising the move to 'new' premises – major because it involved the entire refurbishment of an old mill. Respondent 4 has a strong marketing and selling ability and manages this side of the business. He knows the market and his customers and is able to generate ideas for successful product ranges. Indeed, in these respects, this entrepreneur has much in common with Respondent 11. It is difficult to envisage them delegating this particular responsibility. Furthermore, the crucial function of managing the human resource (both day-to-day and strategically) is an under-developed skill for both Respondents 4 and 11. Henri Strzelecki and Mike Murray both recognised the importance of managing their personnel and they devoted time to doing it and thinking about it. There is some evidence to suggest that Respondents 4 and 11 behave aggressively in their handling of people: Respondent 4 creating friction due to a lack of communication of his ideas and Respondent 11 once having sacked almost his entire shopfloor! Both businesses employ approximately 100 people and for both entrepreneurs this represents a ceiling; they do not want to grow by employing more people. Their identical problem is that being in manufacturing, the choices they have made have meant that growth and expansion are intimately linked with the direct employment of labour. An alternative which was pursued by Respondent 28 is to subcontract the bulk of the manufacture. This option was exercised very successfully by this entrepreneur for a period of four years, although his reasons for making this choice were rather more complex than simply the lack of management skill in handling people.

Within this group of plateauing, established, entrepreneurial businesses, there are other contrasts to be made. It has to be recalled that categorisations at a particular stage of development and growth orientation phase are transient. The expectation is that the Eileen Bilton Partnership (Respondent 25), for example, is likely to move into the professionally-managed category at any time and due to the nature of this particular decision the business is likely to expand rapidly at least in the short term. Respondents 4 and 11, as indicated above, are expected to remain as established, plateaued businesses for the foreseeable future, whereas Respondent 31 is unlikely to stay in the same position for any length of time.

Respondent 31 has a prototypical person profile which is the same as that of Henri Strzelecki, Mike Murray and Respondent 4. Respondent 31 is the type of person who thrives on change and enjoys setting up businesses: he spots an opportunity and moves in quickly to exploit it. His various businesses have usually involved the provision of a service, a minimal capital outlay and low labour costs. It was possible to move out of these businesses as quickly as it was to move into them. In all cases, this entrepreneur set up each business with a partner, jointly operated them for a couple of years and then sold out to the partner. Some time later he would spot another, probably very different, opportunity to make some money and the same thing would happen again. His current business, however, is rather different. It is a new technology-based business venture which has required a large capital outlay necessitating a financial involvement by other parties. The product, which was the respondent's own invention, involves both production and installation. During the four years of life of this business rapid changes have taken place. Initially, he subcontracted much of the work including the installation but this proved to be unsatisfactory because of the lack of reliability. He decided to bring this work in-house resulting in a total labour force of thirty employees, a further problem concerned the marketing of this new product. But the respondent was able to establish himself and this product by high profile activities, including an appearance on a television programme. It soon became clear that another, more sophisticated version of the product was needed if the business was to satisfy customer needs and become a profitable concern. This required another capital injection but the other shareholders were reluctant to make a further investment. Therefore, he had to look elsewhere for the necessary capital. During this period of financial uncertainty he reduced his workforce by one-third. Nevertheless, the company was able to develop and launch a new product and, in addition, was successful in attracting a further injection of capital. At the time of the interview with the respondent it was acknowledged that the company was at a crossroads which could either lead to the realisation of undreamed of success or to bankruptcy.

Summary

By selecting particular cases for illustrative purposes, it has been possible in this section to demonstrate variation within and between the categories. This was especially so for the typology of business owners where the labels used are not universally accepted terms and the categorisation process is difficult. A number of points have been well demonstrated: for example, how people can change their behaviour over the life course and, consequently, 'change' categories. Clearly, phase of life is a major influence on the entrepreneurial personality. Categorisation of the stage of development of the business and growth orientation were less problematic though the transient nature of membership of the categories is well demonstrated. For example, in the case of Eileen Bilton, the phase of post-start-up was almost non-existent and after a very short period, the business is at the category boundary between the established and professionally-managed firm. In addition, arrested growth of the company was a deliberately imposed, temporary situation.

The next section considers the modelling of the categorised data by means of a neural network. Specifically, a network is trained to recognise patterns of attributes and, on the basis of this, business owners and their firms are categorised on the three dimensions. The results of the network are presented and an example given to illustrate its use for prediction purposes.

CATEGORISATION USING NEURAL NETWORKS

The data on the thirty-one business owners were divided into two sets; twenty-five were used as a training set for a neural network, and the remaining six were used to evaluate the performance of the network after training. A three-layer network was used: an input layer, an output layer and one hidden layer. For each of the respondents there are twenty-six input units in the input layer, each corresponding to an attribute as defined in Table 5.1. There are eleven 'target' units in the output layer corresponding to four categories of business owner, three stages of business development and four growth orientations. The target is coded 1 if the respondent, or the firm, is an instance of the category and 0 otherwise (see Table 7.2).

There are several commercially available software packages for analysing neural networks. For our purposes, ANSim version 2.02 (SAIC, 1988) was used to perform a back-propagation to train and test the network. As required by the software, the system was initialised by scaling the input and target vectors and selecting the various parameter values. Scaling was performed so that each input and output element had a value in the interval $(-0.5, 0.5)$ and the weights were set to random numbers in the interval $(-0.3, 0.3)$. The learning parameter was set at 0.1 and the momentum term at 0.6. These values are the default values in ANSim's back-propagation paradigm.

Table 7.2 A definition of the nodes used in a three-layer back-propagation network

Input layer (as defined in Table 5.1)	Hidden layer	Output layer
1. Alert to business opportunities		
2. Pursues opportunity regardless of current resources		
3. Adventurous		
4. Ideas person	1.	
5. Restless/easily bored	2.	
6. High profile image-maker	3.	
7. Proactive	4.	1. Entrepreneur
8. Innovative	5.	2. Quasi-entrepreneur
9. Financial strategy	6.	3. Administrator
10. Has formal minuted meetings	7.	4. Caretaker
11. Roles are clearly defined	.	5. Professionally-managed
12. Has structured strategic plans	.	6. Established
13. Planning is informal	.	7. Post-start-up
14. Employment	.	8. Expanding
15. Age group of owner	.	9. Rejuvenating
16. Age of business	.	10. Plateauing
17. Has previous business experience/ training	.	11. Declining
18. Founded	.	
19. Bought	.	
20. Inherited	.	
21. Has a professional management team		
22. Sons/daughters in the business		
23. Has shown reluctance to change		
24. Wants to grow in numbers employed		
25. Change in employment		
26. Change in floorspace		

Training was performed by presenting to the network each of the twenty-five attribute patterns and repeating this process until some criterion of satisfactory learning had been achieved. After the network classifies an input pattern it is given feedback on the correctness of its output so that the weights on connections between units can be modified. Only after all twenty-five patterns in the training set have been processed are the weights updated. That is, after each complete cycle the weights are adjusted. The network is trained until the maximum unit output error is less than 0.1. Thus, the difference between the trained network outputs and the target outputs never exceeds 0.1.

Table 7.3 Comparison of network properties and prediction results for various sizes of hidden layer

Number of hidden units	Number of connections	Number of cycles	Root mean square error	Proportion of 'failures'
4	163	2977	0.027605	6/66
5	201	1553	0.027601	7/66
6	239	1120	0.028577	6/66
7	277	1341	0.023412	5/66
8	315	1051	0.026014	5/66
12	467	516	0.031679	8/66
16	619	362	0.036637	11/66
20	771	392	0.031598	6/66

The number of hidden units in the intermediate layer of the network was determined empirically. Eight networks, with the number of units in the hidden layer ranging from four to twenty, were trained and compared on the basis of their performance accuracy on the testing set. Each trained network was presented with the input patterns of the six respondents in the testing set and the network's classifications compared with the target categories. An output within 0.1 of the target is deemed to be an accurate prediction, which is the same criterion used when training the network. The number of prediction failures (out of a possible sixty-six) and other details of the eight networks are presented in Table 7.3.

The network with seven hidden units (referred to here as Network 7) was selected on the basis of the lowest proportion of prediction failures combined with the lowest of the eight root mean square errors.

The intelligence of a network is distributed among the weights (and biases) from which predictions can be made for any new input pattern. The weights and biases for Network 7 are presented in Table 7.4, followed by an example of how this is used to classify a respondent from the testing set.

EXAMPLE: CATEGORISATION USING NETWORK 7

Respondent 30 (Don Whitehead of VSW) is selected in order to demonstrate the application of the trained network. His twenty-six input attributes, in their original and scaled form, are listed in Table 7.5.

Table 7.4 Weight and bias matrices for Network 7

Weight matrix – input to hidden layer

```
-0.21 -2.03  1.65  0.09 -1.71 -1.32 -1.51
 0.61  0.50  0.90 -0.61 -0.97  0.89 -0.55
-1.71 -0.33 -0.06  0.45 -0.49 -0.74  1.14
-0.51  0.42 -0.33  0.30 -0.47  0.33 -0.91
-1.23 -1.51  0.42  0.24 -1.94 -1.60  1.47
-1.58  0.74  1.07  0.95  0.55 -2.15  0.26
-0.72 -1.09  4.23 -0.89 -1.02  1.82  1.38
-0.34 -1.10  0.32  1.19  0.88  0.05  1.26
 1.89 -1.89 -0.86  0.08 -0.09 -3.29 -0.89
 0.95 -1.35 -1.57  1.08  1.34 -0.41 -0.29
-1.40  0.43  0.24  1.61 -2.65  0.12  1.87
 1.96  3.21  0.08  1.81 -0.69 -0.97 -1.82
-0.71 -1.36  0.64 -2.42 -0.73  1.73  0.25
 1.30  0.30  0.68  0.99  0.80  0.01  1.43
-0.27 -2.19 -0.59  1.71 -0.19  1.26  0.72
-0.09 -1.36 -1.25  0.47  0.90  0.29  1.38
 1.94 -2.10 -0.98  0.42 -0.35 -1.45 -1.74
 1.23  0.63  2.15  0.18 -0.04  0.18 -1.86
-2.15  0.64 -0.97  0.18  0.19 -0.56  0.85
-0.24 -0.09 -0.63 -0.16 -0.11  0.18  0.14
 0.51  0.70 -0.85  2.61 -0.25 -1.00  2.46
-0.13 -0.91 -0.66  2.16  3.76  0.84  1.52
-0.77  0.84  0.83  1.34  0.87  1.88  0.14
-3.10 -1.03  0.59  1.49  1.87  1.52  1.33
-3.04  2.55  1.29  1.02 -0.99 -0.14  1.22
-2.00  0.65  0.91  1.56 -0.14  0.41  0.93
```

Hidden layer biases

```
1.53 -1.99 -0.13 -0.62 -0.66  0.62  1.67
```

Weight matrix – Hidden to output layer

```
 1.11 -6.60 -1.54  5.17  0.28  0.95 -1.71 -7.11 -1.55  4.98  2.54
-3.03 -0.20 -1.42  3.58  2.31 -8.79  7.25 -0.54 -4.02  2.70  1.29
 6.59  3.92 -8.01 -3.74 -0.35 -0.86  1.82  1.45 -2.51  0.18 -2.43
 0.94 -0.22  2.03 -3.96  7.27 -6.40 -3.60  2.08  3.35 -1.59 -4.98
-1.27  0.87 -1.50  2.95 -0.23 -0.79 -0.41 -5.82  7.75 -1.87 -0.76
-5.15  4.18  5.30  4.62 -2.22  1.78  1.46 -0.78  2.45 -1.98  0.31
-1.97  1.90 -1.07  0.01  2.56 -0.50 -1.83  2.93  0.81 -7.33  5.08
```

Output layer biases

```
-4.18 -3.27 -3.70 -2.66 -0.10 -3.36 -3.57 -2.24 -2.21 -2.17 -5.29
```

Table 7.5 The input pattern for respondent 30 in original and scaled form

Input node	Original input	Scaled input
1	1	0.5
2	1	0.5
3	1	0.5
4	1	0.5
5	1	0.5
6	1	0.5
7	1	0.5
8	3	0.5
9	3	0.5
10	1	0.5
11	1	0.5
12	1	0.5
13	0	−0.5
14	96	−0.26
15	4	0.5
16	14	−0.36
17	1	0.5
18	1	0.5
19	0	−0.5
20	0	−0.5
21	1	0.5
22	1	0.5
23	0	−0.5
24	1	0.5
25	1	0.5
26	1	0.5

Step 1 Multiply the input vector by the weight matrix connecting the input and hidden layers. That is, calculate $Sum = \sum_i x_i w_i$ for each of the 7 nodes in the hidden layer.

$$Sum_1 = 0.50(-0.21) + 0.50(0.61) + 0.50(-1.71) + \ldots$$
$$-\ 0.50(-0.77)\ +\ 0.50(-3.10)\ +\ 0.50(-3.04)$$
$$+\ 0.50(-2.00)$$
$$=\ -1.9456$$

similarly,

$$Sum_2 = -2.4534$$
$$Sum_3 = 4.3732$$
$$Sum_4 = 8.8284$$
$$Sum_5 = -2.4370$$

$Sum_6 = -4.5470$
$Sum_7 = 1.4364$

Step 2 Calculate the *Net* from the input layer to each of the 7 units in the hidden layer. That is, add the hidden layer biases to the summations calculated in step 1.

$Net_1 = -1.9456 + 1.53 = -0.4156$
$Net_2 = -2.4534 - 1.99 = -4.4434$
$Net_3 = 4.3732 - 0.13 = 4.2432$
$Net_4 = 8.8284 - 0.62 = 8.2084$
$Net_5 = -2.4370 - 0.66 = -3.0970$
$Net_6 = -4.5470 + 0.62 = -3.9270$
$Net_7 = 1.4364 + 1.67 = 3.1064$

Step 3 Apply the logistic activation function (which has been modified to take account of the scaling as described in the appendix to chapter 5) to find the activations of each unit in the hidden layer.

$Out_1 = 1/(1+e^{-(-0.4156)}) - 0.5$
$\qquad = -0.102430$

similarly,

$Out_2 = -0.488381$
$Out_3 = 0.485842$
$Out_4 = 0.499728$
$Out_5 = -0.456769$
$Out_6 = -0.480678$
$Out_7 = 0.457156$

Step 4 Calculate the *Sum* for the 11 units in the output layer. That is, multiply the *Out* vector, calculated in Step 3, by the weight matrix connecting the hidden layer to the output layer.

$Sum_1 = -0.102430(1.11) - 0.488381(-3.03) - \ldots$
$\qquad + 0.457156(-1.97)$
$\qquad = 7.19253$

similarly,

$Sum_2 = 1.03025$
$Sum_3 = -4.37750$

$\text{Sum}_4 = -9.63756$
$\text{Sum}_5 = 4.64862$
$\text{Sum}_6 = -0.14386$
$\text{Sum}_7 = -5.63150$
$\text{Sum}_8 = 7.10870$
$\text{Sum}_9 = -1.77064$
$\text{Sum}_{10} = -4.08090$
$\text{Sum}_{11} = -2.03894$

Step 5 Calculate the *Net* from the hidden layer to each of the 11 units in the output layer. That is, add the output layer biases to the summations calculated in Step 4.

$\text{Net}_1 = 7.19253 - 4.18 = 3.01253$
$\text{Net}_2 = 1.03025 - 3.27 = -2.23975$
$\text{Net}_3 = -4.37750 - 3.70 = -8.07750$
$\text{Net}_4 = -9.63756 - 2.66 = -12.29756$
$\text{Net}_5 = 4.64862 - 0.10 = 4.54862$
$\text{Net}_6 = -0.14386 - 3.36 = -3.50386$
$\text{Net}_7 = -5.63150 - 3.57 = -9.20150$
$\text{Net}_8 = 7.10870 - 2.24 = 4.86870$
$\text{Net}_9 = -1.77064 - 2.21 = -3.98064$
$\text{Net}_{10} = -4.08090 - 2.17 = -6.25090$
$\text{Net}_{11} = -2.03894 - 5.29 = -7.32894$

Step 6 Apply the logistic function to find the activation of the 11 units in the output layer. To be consistent these final calculations are expressed correct to 2 places of decimals.

$\text{Out}_1 = 1/(1 + e^{-(3.01253)}) - 0.5$
$= 0.45$

similarly,

$\text{Out}_2 = -0.40$
$\text{Out}_3 = -0.45$
$\text{Out}_4 = -0.50$
$\text{Out}_5 = 0.49$
$\text{Out}_6 = -0.47$
$\text{Out}_7 = -0.50$
$\text{Out}_8 = 0.49$
$\text{Out}_9 = -0.48$
$\text{Out}_{10} = -0.50$
$\text{Out}_{11} = -0.50$

The scaled target outputs for Respondent 30 are respectively:

+0.5 (an entrepreneur)
−0.5 (not a quasi-entrepreneur)
−0.5 (not an administrator)
−0.5 (not a caretaker)
+0.5 (professionally-managed business)
−0.5 (not established)
−0.5 (not post-start-up)
+0.5 (expanding)
−0.5 (not rejuvenating)
−0.5 (not plateauing)
−0.5 (not declining)

Comparing the network outputs with the target outputs demonstrates how well the network has been trained to predict the categorisation of this respondent. All predictions are within 0.1 of the target.

Using a step-by-step approach the above example illustrates how a trained network is used to categorise a new response pattern. Each of the remaining five respondents in the testing set have been categorised by Network 7 in a similar manner. A comparison of the output vectors for the entire testing set as produced by ANSim is given in Table 7.6. Of the five prediction failures (marked in bold), four were unsuccessful in predicting the non-membership of the particular category. However, none of the failures was so extreme as to indicate the opposite to the target. For example, the first scaled target output for Respondent 26 indicates that he is not an entrepreneur (−0.5). Although the predicted output from Network 7 is not within 0.1 of this target, it is nevertheless still a negative prediction. That is, there is no suggestion of this respondent being an entrepreneur. The worst prediction failure is for the eleventh unit of Respondent 29 (not a declining business).

DISCUSSION

The purpose of this chapter was two-fold: first of all, to describe briefly the salient features of a selection of the thirty-one businesses in order to demonstrate the variation within and between the categories; secondly, to illustrate how the knowledge gained by the

Table 7.6　A comparison between the network and target output vectors for the testing set

Network output	Target output	Network output	Target output	Network output	Target output
Respondent 26		**Respondent 27**		**Respondent 28**	
−0.307627	**−0.5**	**−0.311448**	**−0.5**	0.487393	0.5
0.475343	0.5	−0.499991	−0.5	−0.499134	−0.5
−0.498581	−0.5	0.479551	0.5	−0.494180	−0.5
−0.499976	−0.5	−0.489833	−0.5	−0.496077	−0.5
0.440019	0.5	0.456813	0.5	−0.494000	−0.5
−0.420619	−0.5	−0.484630	−0.5	0.483599	0.5
−0.499482	−0.5	−0.499538	−0.5	−0.491451	−0.5
0.498852	0.5	−0.467798	−0.5	−0.470801	−0.5
−0.217047	**−0.5**	−0.494535	−0.5	−0.499886	−0.5
−0.499961	−0.5	0.484717	0.5	0.491642	0.5
−0.499631	−0.5	−0.499350	−0.5	−0.496811	−0.5
Respondent 29		**Respondent 30**		**Respondent 31**	
−0.499963	−0.5	0.453078	0.5	0.493282	0.5
−0.458752	−0.5	−0.403625	−0.5	−0.499666	−0.5
−0.483041	−0.5	−0.451582	−0.5	−0.481608	−0.5
0.481254	0.5	−0.499994	−0.5	−0.498839	−0.5
−0.477620	−0.5	0.489539	0.5	−0.423120	−0.5
0.484378	0.5	−0.470724	−0.5	**0.364373**	**0.5**
−0.499264	−0.5	−0.499899	−0.5	−0.497936	−0.5
−0.499132	−0.5	0.492302	0.5	−0.464627	−0.5
0.491240	0.5	−0.481647	−0.5	−0.499728	−0.5
−0.499136	−0.5	−0.498066	−0.5	0.492035	0.5
−0.028329	**−0.5**	−0.499338	−0.5	−0.499401	−0.5

research team and the methodology adopted can be used to train a neural network to recognise and predict category membership of respondents on the basis of their response pattern to a set of attributes.

A not untypical caretaker may operate a small but stable business; it exploits a niche and perhaps offers a service which no-one else, particularly a larger business, is prepared to do. On the other hand, caretakers might manage medium-sized or even large businesses. This might seem counter-intuitive where the caretaker was the founder. It suggests the importance of taking into account the stage in life of the individual: a social learning theory of personality development suggests that it is quite possible to lose those entrepreneurial attributes which were critical in the early stages of the development of the business. Caretakers may also find themselves at the helm of a business which requires them to behave in a manner unsuited to their personality. The circumstance which precipitated this turn of events may have been outside their control, although their lack of entrepreneurial adroitness is likely to have contributed to their inability to see it coming. The key entrepreneurial attribute in this situation is what we have termed 'proactivity' which includes anticipation and foresight.

Administrators are quite capable of developing sound businesses, although they tend to do it without the flair of an entrepreneur. For example, they are not particularly adventurous in their business plans or the vision they have for their enterprise. They tend to react to changed circumstances rather than nose out opportunities. Depending upon the size and age of the business, they are likely to have developed formal structures to cope with the administration of the business. They believe in the commitment of resources to the business and invest where logic dictates.

The quasi-entrepreneurs did have many of the characteristics of the entrepreneur, but they were less opportunistic and not as adventurous or imaginative in their financial strategy. However, this has to be qualified by consideration of other factors. For example, a post-start-up firm does not have the same scope to exploit a wide variety of sources of finance.

The entrepreneurs fell into two groups. One group comprised founders of well-established, professionally-managed businesses which were, nevertheless still growing and developing. The other group of younger businesses was quite a 'mixed bag'. Two of the business owners in the latter group had found themselves up against the transition threshold: if they were to develop the company further they would have to bring about changes which involved delegation and the development of a professional management team. This meant sacrificing the tasks they enjoyed most, taking on different responsibilities and operating in a way which was quite alien to them. Both had arrested the development of their companies at that threshold. One Managing Director had expressed no intention of taking that business any further and was looking around for other business ideas. It is uncertain what will happen in the other case. It is clear, however, that the management of the human resource is also a critical element in the development of entrepreneurial businesses as Henri Strzelecki and Mike Murray have demonstrated. It takes more than a dim awareness if the

management and development of personnel is to be done effectively, it is a skill which has to be recognised, developed and worked
at.

The stage of development and growth orientation categories were
also shown to be critical in differentiating between the companies.
The Eileen Bilton Partnership was seen to be in transit and, unlike
the situation of Respondent 4, was being prepared to cross the
boundary and become a professionally-managed business. Finally,
Respondent 31's new business venture shows the precarious nature
of entrepreneurial activity and that having all the 'right' personal
characteristics does not guarantee successful business performance.

Artificial neural networks were introduced in chapter 5 as an
appropriate tool for pattern recognition and categorisation with
'soft' data. This is particularly so when attempting to classify people
on the basis of complex patterns of behaviour.

The latter part of this chapter has been devoted to the
development of a neural network that has been trained to perform
the three-fold categorisation. A three-layered network architecture
was defined, with twenty-six input nodes corresponding to the
twenty-six attributes, and eleven output nodes. The network was
trained with data from twenty-five of the respondents and tested by
means of its predictive performance on the remaining six. Indeed,
the 'optimal' number of units in the hidden layer was determined
according to this predictive performance criterion in conjunction
with the minimum total root mean square error.

Network 7 successfully predicts sixty-one out of the sixty-six
required categorisations according to the acceptance criterion
imposed. However, the analysis was far from exhaustive and the
predictive power and speed of training of Network 7 could well be
improved by a different choice of parameters. In addition, an
enlarged training set with wider coverage of the categories would
present the network with greater 'knowledge' on which to base its
predictions.

8 Epilogue

Sexton's critique of entrepreneurship research suggested that much of what has been reported has 'reinvented the wheel' and that, consequently, little progress is evident (Sexton, 1987). This is a harsh criticism but serves to stimulate debate and fundamental rethinking. The questioning of the conceptual basis of such research has indicated the need for an innovative approach. As a consequence, in this monograph, we have sought to ask fundamental questions about possible approaches which have encompassed:

1 a consideration of the contribution of economics to the development of an understanding of the psychology of the entrepreneur;
2 a reconceptualisation of the basic terminology, in particular, entrepreneurs versus business owners in general;
3 the adoption of a holistic approach, using principally a biographical method with a spectrum of actual business owners;
4 the categorisation of owners and their businesses using the concept of 'prototypicality';
5 the application of neural networks for training and prediction purposes.

In this chapter the implications of these points for further refinements to the methodology adopted in our field study will be discussed. This clears the way for a restatement of the position taken on the nature of the entrepreneurial personality.

REFINEMENTS TO THE METHODOLOGY

The contribution of economics

Economists have opened up a field rich in psychological concepts in order to further the understanding of entrepreneurs and entrepreneurship. This impression is reinforced by the evidence presented in chapter 2. However, the dearth of psychologists mining such wealth is evidenced by the scant reference to the subject in a book purporting to describe the economic mind (Furnham and Lewis, 1986). Bridging this divide is not only a challenge but there are rich pickings to be had.

A recently-published work adds grist to the mill. Binks and Vale (1990) distinguish between three types of economic event. Such events have implications for the nature of the opportunity open to the business owner. The typology comprises: catalytic, allocating and refining event. The *catalytic event* is inspired by Schumpeter's concept of innovation which he construes as bringing together 'new combinations'. This is the 'genuinely new' instigated with 'the uncertain prospect of monopoly profit' (Binks and Vale, 1990, p.41). The *allocating event* occurs as a consequence of the catalytic. That is, innovation creates market opportunities which the alert entrepreneur will then exploit. The *refining event*, however, is rather different. This concerns the optimal or efficient allocation of resources. Competitive pressures, for example, will result in attempts to increase efficiency of plant and the human resource. Endeavours to strike productivity deals or to purchase the latest technology in order to increase efficiency are instances of refining activities.

In practice, it may be difficult to identify a truly catalytic event until the impact upon the industry becomes evident. Certainly, Binks and Vale emphasise, it does not mean simply founding a 'new' business; it is a transforming process. Entrepreneurs who can engage in such activity undoubtedly are rare, but there are many more who can spot the opportunities to be exploited in the wake of such an event. Both catalytic and allocative events and their associated activities are consonant with the defining characteristics of the entrepreneurs described in this monograph. The refining event and the behaviours appropriate to it are reminiscent of the prototypical behaviour of the administrator. Further, it would seem that business owners may engage in a mix of catalytic, allocating and refining behaviours. The former behaviour is *unlikely* to be a part of the repertoire of the caretaker. Allocating and refining behaviours are more common, though the latter more so under competitive conditions.

Reconceptualisation of the basic terminology

Much previous research has tended to treat the terms 'entrepreneur' and 'business owner' or 'owner-manager' as if they were equivalent. Indeed, an entrepreneur is also often equated with being a founder

(Haworth, 1988; Ginsberg and Buchholtz, 1989). The conflation of terms such as these has led to impoverished research which has served only to confuse. To pursue an even more trenchant line of argument, research purporting to identify the characteristics of entrepreneurs by pursuing a univariate approach might be criticised as being far too simplistic. An entrepreneur cannot be distinguished from a non-entrepreneur on the basis of one characteristic or trait. There is a set of interacting characteristics which requires simul-taneous investigation. There are several studies of constellations of entrepreneurial personality traits (see, for example, Churchill, 1983; McClelland, 1987; Meredith *et al.*, 1982; Timmons, 1989), but they do not provide an identical set. The set of attributes used to define the 'entrepreneur' category in this research was similarly based upon a combination of scholarship and experience and there was no *a priori* assumption of the number of other categories of business owner that might be differentiated.

Given a set of attributes or traits, a related issue is how they might be conceived and 'measured'. The line of argument pursued in this monograph is that traits are categorising concepts which organise and make sense of actual behaviour observed from multiple perspectives (Hampson, 1988). It assumes consistency in the manifestation of behaviour in like situations and the ability to explain observed inconsistencies. It suggests the need to use methods whereby observations can be made on different occasions from the perspective of different observers in a range of relevant situations. Furthermore, behaviours were assumed to be prototypi-cal of a particular trait, but not exclusively so, that is they could be overlapping and prototypical of more than one trait. This was due to the high co-occurrence of many of these trait terms. The selection of such attributes is an aspect of the research where further work needs to be done.

The holistic approach

The biographical approach enables the observation and categorisa-tion of the individual's behaviour in context, but there are practical difficulties with this method. It is time-consuming and resource-intensive, requiring considerable technical skill in its administration to ensure that reliability and validity are maintained. The challenge for further research is how to reduce this particular method to manageable proportions. One issue is whether to continue to use the biographical method or to adopt a method akin to the act frequency approach of Buss and Craik (Buss and Craik, 1980, 1981, 1983). The problem with adopting the latter method is being able to nominate a sufficiently comprehensive and representative list of acts which can be used across all businesses. Formulating such a list for entrepreneurial behaviours would be a project in itself.

At the attribute level further consideration is whether it would be better to develop more inclusive categories or to disaggregate them further. The argument for greater inclusiveness – a form of superordinate level categorisation – would be that the behaviours of business owners should not be excluded from particular category membership due to the narrowness of our categories. However, categories vary quite naturally with respect to their breadth. It does not appear that the continued use of concepts like opportunistic, innovative, imaginative, restless, etc., is presenting this kind of problem. The superordinate level category for these concepts implicitly is 'entrepreneurial'. On the other hand, further research might enable the identification of more specific behaviours (subordinate level categories) which typify the particular category of business owner.

Categorisation procedure

The sufficiency of the evidence to enable the categorisation process to take place will always be a matter of judgement. However, to reduce the subjective nature of this process, two criteria have been espoused. They are consistency and frequency. A very clear example of the use of these criteria was in the categorisation of Respondent 13 in chapter 7. He had behaved entrepreneurially on one recent occasion and it was indisputably an entrepreneurial act. However, this particular business owner did not consistently behave in such a manner, quite the contrary in fact; it was alien to his personality so to do. He had felt forced to make such a change in the direction of the business through circumstances outside his control.

Due to the definitional problems alluded to in the first chapter, we have had to use categories of business owner which are not in everyday use (that is, they are not 'natural' categories). A similar criticism was levelled at Cantor and Mischel's work on person categorisation (see Hampson, 1988, p.202). The lack of universally accepted categories of business owner is an inhibiting factor.

Despite this, subordinate level categories of 'business owner' could be defined. The evidence for this assertion is the variation which was found within the person categories investigated. For example within the category 'entrepreneur' it was possible to distinguish between those who were 'task-oriented' and those who were 'people-oriented'. The former tended to lack the organisation management skills to allow the firm to grow beyond a certain size threshold. This raises the question of whether in addition to the skills constraint there is also an associated personality constraint.

The question might arise as to why in a book purporting to describe the entrepreneurial personality there is a need to single out and categorise two dimensions pertaining to the business. The two dimensions – stage of development of the business and growth orientation – were introduced because it was felt that they reflect critical aspects of the business situation. With a larger sample size it would be possible to investigate formally the association between types of business owner and these two dimensions. Start-up businesses were deliberately omitted. The three stages termed post-start-up, established and professionally-managed were defined largely by the degree of formality of procedures and the extent of the management team. It was assumed that at the different stages, the problems to be tackled by the business owner would change and with that would come a change in behaviour. The data gleaned suggest that it would be possible to deduce whether or not the business owner was adjusted to a particular stage and/or able to accommodate to demands brought about by further development.

The success of an enterprise can be an added source of confusion when labelling the business owner an 'entrepreneur' or otherwise. That is, an enterprise may be profitable but not an entrepreneurially-led concern. Thus, the idea that an entrepreneurially-led business is necessarily successful is clearly unacceptable. It was therefore thought important to separate out some measure of success. Not surprisingly, studies which have attempted to take account of this factor have tended to use financial ratios as *the* measure of performance. The problems with this approach are that: (1) there is no one ratio which is adequate for the task and it is often difficult to quantify trends over time; (2) small businesses (as defined by the Companies Act 1985) are exempt from certain disclosures and are not obliged to submit a profit and loss account; (3) there is a need to compare ratios with an industry standard in order to be able to interpret a particular performance as being above or below average. The adoption of a measure termed growth orientation avoids these problems and incorporates not only aspects of the business context but also attitude to growth.

The application of neural networks

It is thought that the method adopted in this research is quite distinctive, drawing on relatively recent developments in personality theory and categorisation processes. The application of artificial neural networks adds yet another innovation. Neural networks function in a way which is reminiscent of human cognitive processes. As such they may be applied to a wide range of pattern recognition tasks and are able to learn from experience and to generalise and abstract. This, plus the capability of 'seeing through' noise and distortion in patterns obtained from real-world situations, enables the development of a knowledge base which can be stored, built upon and used for prediction purposes.

Back-propagation is the most widely used of the training algorithms but it is not without its problems. There is no guarantee that the network will train to the best configuration possible. That is, the algorithm may find a local rather than a global solution. Given the complexity of the connections and the fact that many operations are being computed simultaneously, it is often very difficult to know what is going on in the network. It is not possible to test the significance of the inputs as when applying traditional statistical procedures. The choice of initial values for the various training parameters and the number of units in the hidden layer(s) appears to be somewhat arbitrary and demands a considerable degree of trial and error. However, some of these problems may be reduced, if not eliminated, as more research is pursued in this field.

Despite these apparent disadvantages we believe that we have demonstrated the enormous potential for the application of neural networks to problems with a strong psychological flavour. The method readily accommodates imprecision; it takes all the information (inputs) into account simultaneously and so the interaction between variables is implicit within the system.

THE ENTREPRENEURIAL PERSONALITY

The idea that trait terms can be construed as 'natural categories' has presented an opportunity to apply a distinct and original framework to research which seeks to characterise the entrepreneurial personality. This means that trait descriptors can be employed which explicitly acknowledge and assimilate a lay perspective. For example, to be *enterprising* is to be: pioneering, adventurous, venturesome, daring, go-ahead, progressive, innovative. The language is rich in such naturally, co-occurring descriptors. This is not to construe the technical terminology of personality theory as if it were solely an instrument of language. On the contrary, trait terms, such as 'adventurous', 'innovative', 'opportunistic', etc. do have referents and these are the varied behavioural acts of the individual.

This approach resolves a number of difficulties which have manifested themselves in previous research. It casts further doubt on the use of psychometric tests (especially where they have been devised for other purposes) to identify entrepreneurial traits. It nullifies the objections of writers such as Stevenson (see chapter 4) who is dismissive of research purporting to identify the personality characteristics of entrepreneurs. This is because the holistic approach we have adopted is not concerned with statistical descriptions and summaries of the presence or absence of so-called entrepreneurial traits in given populations. Rather, it enables connections to be made between meaningful behavioural acts and the personality characteristics of the incumbent. Also, due to the fact that accounts of behaviour are given in context, detailed explanations of the incumbent's behaviour are possible. This level of analysis is enriched by the option of proffering such explanations from the multiple perspectives of different observers. Contradictions may be resolved, or at least recognised, and evidence of cross-situational specificity and consistency in behaviours may be assembled. Further, the accounts given of their own behaviour enable the exploration of the cognitive structures of the individual business owner. This is crucially important in examining relationships such as that between behaviour and stage of development of the business. Other dimensions which have not been investigated systematically in this research are the relationship between age, past experience, gender and the personality of the business owner.

The adoption of a lay perspective means, at one level of understanding, that, of course, people have always known what entrepreneurs are, but only *implicitly*. This understanding has been rendered explicit in this research. However, it was not an objective of the present research to consider the impact of a cultural perspective on interpretations of the entrepreneurial personality. This is clearly a fruitful area for further research.

Using terms like 'opportunistic', 'innovative', 'adventurous' to label aspects of entrepreneurial behaviour suggests that the latter is a multi-faceted construct. In terms of current thinking, the term 'entrepreneurial' is a relatively broad categorising concept. It stands in hierarchical relationship to such lower order traits. Our prototypical entrepreneur therefore is *opportunistic*, *innovative*, *imaginative*, an *ideas-person*, an *agent of change*, *restless*, *adventurous*, *proactive* and *adopts a broad financial strategy*. There is some overlap between these trait terms which means that care is needed in the interpretation and categorisation of their behavioural manifestations. For instance, the pursuit of a particular business strategy might suggest both imagination and vision, so too might the development of a particular innovation or the pursuit of a particular opportunity. Further, the entrepreneur's ability to generate ideas might be managed by adopting the role of catalyst. A combination of imagination, awareness of an opportunity and adventurousness ensures that the entrepreneur takes the idea further. The interaction between such traits demonstrates the need to think of the entrepreneurial personality as a complex set of traits.

Is the quasi-entrepreneur, perhaps, a non-prototypical entrepreneur? Would such an assumption not simplify our categorisation of business owners? Clearly it would. The quasi-entrepreneur is at the fuzzy boundary between the entrepreneur and the administrator. However, whilst entrepreneurs are alive to opportunities with an eye to the main chance, quasi-entrepreneurs do not follow this through with the same conviction, a conviction indicated by their pursuit of the opportunity regardless of resources currently controlled. They thus have a tendency to let opportunities go. This seems to 'dilute' other aspects of their otherwise entrepreneurial behaviour. It means, for example, that they are adventurous to a point; that they may be imaginative, but not in all areas of business activity, and so on. A fitting analogy taken from the 'object world' is that of the patio-window/patio-door. The quasi-entrepreneur nevertheless warrants separate categorisation.

CONCLUDING STATEMENT

It is inevitable when attempting to break new ground that one's work will be closely scrutinised and possibly heavily criticised. The research that we have undertaken and reported is of an exploratory nature and clearly in need of further refinements. What we have presented is a framework and a new set of tools for setting about the task. Indeed, when we cast our minds back to the sentiments neatly encapsulated in the concept of 'hunting the Heffalump', we believe that we have made considerable strides forward. However, we discovered that 'hunting' was not the way to capture the entrepreneur; fishing was likely to be a more rewarding pastime! Like shoals of fish, business owners are many and various. Trawling them using a wide net in deep and dark waters is perhaps a more fitting analogy to the task we have undertaken. Further research will, we believe, capture the entrepreneur – in a neural net!

Bibliography

ALEKSANDER, I. and MORTON, H. (1990) *An Introduction to Neural Computing*, London: Chapman & Hall.

ALDRICH, H. and ZIMMER, C. (1986) 'Entrepreneurship through social networks', in D. L. Sexton and R. W. Smilor (eds) *The Art and Science of Entrepreneurship*, Cambridge, Mass.: Ballinger: 2–23.

ANDERSON, J. A. and ROSENFELD, E. (1988) *Neurocomputing: Foundations of Research*, Cambridge, Mass.: MIT Press.

ANGLEITNER, A. and DEMTRODER, A. I. (1988) 'Acts and dispositions: a reconsideration of the act frequency approach', *European Journal of Personality*, 2: 121–41.

ARGYLE, M. and LITTLE, B. (1972) 'Do personality traits apply to social behaviour?', *Journal for the Theory of Social Behaviour*, 2, 1:1–35.

ATKINSON, R. H. and BIRCH, D. (1979) *Introduction to Motivation*, New Jersey: Van Nostrand.

BECHHOFER, F. and ELLIOTT, B. (1976) 'Persistence and change: the petite bourgeoisie in industrial society', *European Journal of Sociology*, XVII, 2: 74–99.

BECHHOFER, F. and ELLIOTT, B. (eds) (1981) *The Petite Bourgeoisie, Comparative Studies of the Uneasy Stratum*, London: Macmillan.

BEGLEY, T. M. and BOYD, D. P. (1985) 'The relationship of the Jenkins Activity Survey to Type A behaviour and business executives', *Journal of Vocational Behaviour*, 27: 316–28.

BEGLEY, T. M and BOYD, D. P (1986) 'Psychological characteristics associated with entrepreneurial performance', in R. Ronstadt, J. A. Hornaday, R. Peterson and K. H. Vesper, (eds) *Frontiers of Entrepreneurship Research*, Wellesley, Mass.: Babson College, Center for Entrepreneurial Studies: 146–65.

BINKS, M. and VALE, P. (1990) *The Rise and Decline of Small Firms*, London: Allen & Unwin.

BOYD, D. P (1984) 'Type A behaviour, financial performance and organizational growth in small business firms', *Journal of Occupational Psychology*, 57:137–40.

BROCKHAUS, R. H. (1980a) 'Psychological and environmental factors which distinguish the successful from the unsuccessful entrepreneur: a longitudinal study', paper submitted to the Academy of Management Meeting.

BROCKHAUS, R. H. (1980b) 'Risk taking propensity of entrepreneurs', *Academy of Management Journal*, 23, 3: 509–20.

BROCKHAUS, R. H. (1982) 'The psychology of the entrepeneur', in C. A. Kent, D. .L. Sexton and K. H. Vesper, (eds) *Encyclopedia of Entrepreneurship*, Englewood-Cliffs, N.J.: Prentice-Hall.

BROCKHAUS, R. H. and HORWITZ, P. S. (1986) 'The psychology of the entrepreneur', in D. L. Sexton and R. W. Smilor, (eds) *The Art and Science of Entrepreneurship*, Cambridge, Mass.: Ballinger: 25–48.

BROCKHAUS, R. H. and NORD, W. R. (1979) 'An exploration of factors affecting the entrepreneurial decision: personal characteristics vs. environmental conditions', *Proceedings of the National Academy of Management*.

BURNS, B. and KIPPENBERGER, A. (1988) *Entrepreneur*, London: Macmillan.

BURNS, T. and STALKER, G. M. (1961) *The Management of Innovation*, London: Tavistock.

BUSS, D. M. and CRAIK, K. H. (1980) 'The frequency approach of disposition: dominance and prototypically dominant acts', *Journal of Personality*, 48: 379–92.

BUSS, D. M. and CRAIK, K. H. (1981) 'The act frequency analysis of interpersonal dispositions: aloofness, gregariousness, dominance, and submissiveness', *Journal of Personality*, 49: 174–92.

BUSS, D. M. and CRAIK, K. H. (1983) 'The act frequency approach to personality', *Psychology Review*, 90: 105–26.

CANTILLON, R. (1755) *Essai sur la nature du commerce en général*. Ed. by H. Higgs, London: Macmillan, 1931.

CANTOR, N. and MISCHEL, W. (1979) 'Prototypes in person perception', *Advances in Experimental Social Psychology*, 12: 3–52.

CARLAND, J. W., HOY, F., BOULTON, W. R., CARLAND, J. A. C. (1984) 'Differentiating entrepreneurs from small business owners: a conceptualization', *Academy of Management Review*, 9, 2: 354–9.

CARSRUD, A. L., OLM, K. W., and EDDY, G. G. (1986) 'Entrepreneurship: research in quest of a paradigm', in D. L. Sexton and R. W. Smilor (eds) *The Art and Science of Entrepreneurship*, Cambridge, Mass.: Ballinger: 367–78.

CASSON, M. (1982) *The Entrepreneur – An Economic Theory*, Oxford: Martin Robertson.

CHELL, E. (1985) 'The entrepreneurial personality: a few ghosts laid to rest?', *International Small Business Journal*, 3, 3: 43–54.

CHELL, E. (1986) 'The entrepreneurial personality: a review and some theoretical developments', in J. Curran, *et al.* (eds) *The Survival of the Small Firm, Vol. 1: The Economics of Survival and Entrepreneurship*, Aldershot: Gower: 102–19.

CHELL, E. and HAWORTH, J. M. (1986) 'A study of the factors affecting the sales performance of independent retail newsagents', in A. Gibb, *et al.* (eds) *Small Firms; Needs, Resources and Proceedings*, London: Gower.

CHELL, E. and HAWORTH, J. M. (1987) 'Entrepreneurship and the Entrepreneurial Pesonality: a review', *London Business School Small Business Bibliography 1985–86*.

CHELL, E. and HAWORTH, J. M. 1988 'Entrepreneurship and entrepreneurial management: the need for a paradigm', *Graduate Management Research*, 4, 1: 16–33.

CHURCHILL, N. C. (1983) 'Entrepreneurs and their enterprises: a stage model', in J. A. Hornaday, J. A. Timmons, and K. H. Vesper, (eds) *Frontiers of Entrepreneurship Research*, Wellesley, Mass.: Babson College, Center for Entrepreneurial Studies: 1–22.

CLARK, J. B. (1907) *Essentials of Economic Theory*, repr. (1968) New York: Augustus M. Kelley.

COCHRAN, T. C. (1969) 'Entrepreneurship', in D. L. Sills (ed.) *International Encyclopedia of the Social Sciences* 5, New York: Macmillan and The Free Press: 87–90.

COOPER, A. C. (1982) 'The entrepreneurship – small business interface', in C. A. Kent, D. L. Sexton, and K. H. Vesper, *Encyclopedia of Entrepreneurship*, Englewood-Cliffs, N.J.: Prentice-Hall, 10: 193–208.

COVIN, J. G. and SLEVIN, D. P. (1986) 'The development and testing of an organizational-level entrepreneurship scale', in R. Ronstadt, J. A. Hornaday, R. Peterson and K. A. Vesper, (eds) *Frontiers of Entrepreneurship Research*, Wellesley, Mass.: Babson College, Center for Entrepreneurial Studies: 628–39.

COVIN, J. G. and SLEVIN, D. P. (1988) 'The influence of organization structure on the utility of an entrepreneurial top management style', *Journal of Management Studies*, 25, 3: 217–34.

COVIN, J. G. and SLEVIN, D. P. (1989) 'The strategic management of small firms in hostile and benign environments', *Strategic Management Journal*, 10: 75–87.

D'ANDRADE, R. G. (1974) 'Meaning and the assessment of behavior', in H. M. Blalock Jr. (ed.) *Measurement in the Social Sciences*, Chicago: Aldine–Atherton.

DICKIE-CLARK, H. P. (1966) *The Marginal Situation*, London: Routledge & Kegan Paul.

DUNKELBERG, W. C and COOPER, A. C. (1982) 'Entrepreneurial typologies: an empirical study', in K. H. Vesper (ed.) *Frontiers of Entrepreneurial Research*, Wellesley, Mass.: Babson College, Center for Entrepreneurial Studies: 1–15.

ENDLER, N. and MAGNUSSON, D. (1976) 'Toward an interactional psychology of personality', *Psychological Bulletin*, 83, 5: 956–74.

FILLEY, A. C. and ALDAG, R. J. (1978) 'Characteristics and measurement of an organizational typology', *Academy of Management Journal*, 21, 4: 576–91.

FLAMHOLTZ, E. G. (1986) *How to Make the Transition from an Entrepreneurship to a Professionally Managed Firm*, San Francisco: Jossey-Bass.

FLANAGAN, J. C. (1954) 'The critical incident technique', *Psychological Bulletin*, 15: 327–58.

FURNHAM, A. (1986) 'Economic locus of control', *Human Relations*, 39, 1: 29–43.

FURNHAM, A. and LEWIS, A. (1986) *The Economic Mind – The Social Psychology of Economic Behaviour*, Brighton: Wheatsheaf.

GIBB, A. and RITCHIE, J. (1981) 'Influences on entrepreneurship: a study over time', *Bolton Ten Years On – Proceedings of the UK Small Business Research Conference*, Nov. 20–21, Polytechnic of Central London.

GIBB, A. & RITCHIE, J. (1982) 'Understanding the process of starting small business', *European Small Business Journal*, 1, 1: 26–45.

GINSBERG, A. and BUCHHOLTZ, A. (1989), 'Are entrepreneurs a breed apart? a look at the evidence', *Journal of General Management*, 15, 2: 32–40.

GOFFEE, R. and SCASE, R. (1985) *Women in Charge – The Experiences of Female Entrepreneurs*, London: Allen & Unwin.

HAMPSON, S. E. (1982) *The Construction of Personality*, London: Routledge & Kegan Paul.

HAMPSON, S. E. (1984) 'Personality traits: in the eye of the beholder or the personality of the perceived?' in M. Cook (ed.) *Psychology in Progress: Issues in Person Perception*, London: Methuen.

HAMPSON, S. E. (1988) *The Construction of Personality*, 2nd ed. London: Routledge.

HAMPSON, S. E., JOHN, O. P. and GOLDBERG, L. R. (1986) 'Category breadth and hierarchical structure in personality: studies of asymmetries in judgements of trait implications', *Journal of Personality and Social Psychology*, 51: 37–54.

HARWOOD, E. (1982) 'The sociology of entrepreneurship', in C. A. Kent, *et al.* (eds) *Encyclopedia of Entrepreneurship*, Englewood-Cliffs, N.J.: Prentice-Hall.

HAWORTH, J. M. (1988) *An Investigation of Entrepreneurial Characteristics using Latent Class Analysis*, unpublished Ph.D. Thesis, Department of Business and Management Studies, University of Salford.

HEBB, D. O. (1949) *The Organization of Behavior*, New York: Wiley.

HÉBERT, R. F. and LINK, A. N. (1988) *The Entrepreneur – Mainstream Views and Radical Critiques*, 2nd ed. New York: Praeger.

HETTEMA, P. J. and KENRICK, D. T. (1989) 'Biosocial interaction and individual adaptation', in P. J. Hettema, (ed.) *Personality and Environment: Assessment of Human Adaptation*, Chichester, England: Wiley.

HORNADAY, J. A. and ABOUD, J. (1971) 'Characteristics of successful entrepreneurs', *Personnel Psychology*, 24: 141–53.

HOY, F. and CARLAND, J. W. (1983) 'Differentiating between entrepreneurs and small business owners in new venture formation', in J. A. Hornaday, J. A. Timmons and K. H. Vesper, (eds) *Frontiers of Entrepreneurship Research*, Wellesley, Mass.: Babson College, Center for Entrepreneurial Studies: 157–66.

HULL, D. L., BOSLEY, J. J. and UDELL, G. G. (1980) 'Renewing the hunt for the heffalump: identifying potential entrepreneurs by personality characteristics', *Journal of Small Business*, 18, 1: 11–18.

JULIAN, J. W., LICHTMAN, C. M. and RYCKMAN, R. M. (1968) 'Internal-external control and need to control', *Journal of Social Psychology*, 76: 43–8.

KAZANJIAN, R. K. (1984) 'Operationalising stage of growth: an empirical assessment of dominant problems', in J. A. Hornaday, F.

Tarpley, J. A. Timmons, and K. H. Vesper (eds) *Frontiers of Entrepreneurship Research*, Wellesley, Mass.: Babson College, Center for Entrepreneurial Studies: 144–58.

KENRICK, D. T. and FUNDER, D. C. (1988) 'Profiting from controversy: lessons from the person-situation debate', *American Psychologist*, 43, 1: 23–34.

KETS DE VRIES, M. F. R. (1977) 'The entrepreneurial personality: a person at the crossroads', *Journal of Management Studies*, (Feb.): 34–57.

KILBY, P. M. (ed.) (1971) *Entrepreneurship and Economic Development*, New York: Macmillan.

KIRZNER, I. M. (1982) 'The theory of entrepreneurship in economic growth', in C. A. Kent, D. L. Sexton and K. H. Vesper, *Encyclopedia of Entrepreneurship*, Englewood Cliffs, N.J.: Prentice-Hall.

KLINE, P. (1986) *A Handbook of Test Construction: Introduction to Psychometric Design*, New York: Methuen.

KNIGHT, F. H. (1921) *Risk, Uncertainty and Profit,* New York: Houghton Mifflin.

KOESTLER, A. (1964) *Act of Creation*, London: Hutchinson.

LESSEM, R. (1986a) *Enterprise Development*, Aldershot: Gower.

LESSEM, R. (1986b) 'Becoming a metrapreneur', *Journal of General Management*, 11, 4:5–21.

LEVENSON, H. (1973) 'Multidimensional locus of control in psychiatric patients', *Journal of Consulting and Clinical Psychology*, 41, 3: 397–404.

LEVINE, R. (1966) *Dreams and Deeds: Achievement Motivation in Nigeria*, Chicago Press.

LEVINSON, D. J. (1978) *The Seasons of a Man's Life*, New York: Knopf.

LIPPMANN, R. P. (1987) 'An introduction to computing with neural nets', *IEEE ASSP Magazine*, April: 4–22.

LIVESAY, H. C. (1982) 'Entrepreneurial history', in C. A. Kent, D. L. Sexton and K. H. Vesper (eds) *Encyclopedia of Entrepreneurship*, Englewood-Cliffs, N.J.: Prentice-Hall.

McCLELLAND, D. C. (1961) *The Achieving Society*, Princeton, N.J.: Van Nostrand.

McCLELLAND, D. C. (1965) 'Achievement motivation can be developed', *Harvard Business Review*, 43: 6–24, 178.

McCLELLAND, D. C. (1987) 'Characteristics of successful entrepreneurs', *Journal of Creative Behavior*, 21, 3: 219–33.

McCLELLAND, D. C. and WINTER, D. G. (1971) *Motivating Economic Achievement*, New York: Free Press.

MAGNUSSON, D. (ed.) (1981) *Toward a Psychology of Situations – An Interactional Perspective*, Hillsdale, N.J.: Lawrence Erlbaum Associates.

MARSHALL, A. (1920) *Principles of Economics*, 8th ed. London: Macmillan.

MEREDITH, G. G., NELSON, R. E. and NECK, P. A. (1982) *The Practice of Entrepreneurship*, Geneva: International Labour Office.

MILL, J. S. (1965) *Principles of Political Economy,* London: Routledge & Kegan Paul. Books 1–5.

MILLER, D. (1983) 'The correlates of entrepreneurship in three types of firms', *Management Science*, 29, 7: 770–91.

MILLER, D. and FRIESEN, P. H. (1982) 'Innovation in conservative and entrepreneurial firms: two models of strategic momentum', *Strategic Management Journal*, 3: 1–25.

MILLER, D. and FRIESEN, P. H. (1984) *Organizations – A Quantum View*, Englewood Cliffs, N.J.: Prentice Hall.

MILLER, D. and TOULOUSE, J.-M. (1986) 'Chief executive personality and corporate strategy and structure in small firms', *Management Science*, 32, 11: 1389–409.

MINTZBERG, H. (1979) *The Structuring of Organizations: A Synthesis of the Research*, Englewood Cliffs, N.J.: Prentice Hall.

MIRON, D. and McCLELLAND, D. C. (1979) 'The impact of achievement motivation training on small business performance', *California Management Review*, 21, 4: 13–28.

MISCHEL, W. (1968) *Personality and Assessment*, New York: Wiley.

MISCHEL, W. (1973) 'Towards a cognitive social learning reconceptualisation of personality', *Psychological Review*, 80, 4: 252–83.

MISES, L. VON, (1949) *Human Action: A Treatise on Economics*, New Haven, CT.: Yale University Press.

NORRIS, K. (1984) 'Small building firms – their origins, characteristics and development needs', paper presented to the *Seventh National Small Firms Policy and Research Conference*, Sept. 5–7, Trent Polytechnic, Nottingham.

PALMER, M. (1971) 'The application of pscyhological testing to entrepreneurial potential', *California Management Review*, XIII, 3: 32–8.

RICARDO, D. (1962) *The Principles of Political Economy and Taxation*, Letchworth: Aldine Press.

RICKETTS, M. (1987) *The Economics of Business Enterprise – New Approaches to the Firm*, Brighton: Wheatsheaf.

ROSCH, E., MERVIS, C. B., GRAY, W. D., JOHNSON, D. M. and BOYES-BREAM, P. (1976) 'Basic objects in natural categories', *Cognitive Psychology*, i: 332–439.

ROSCH, E. (1978) 'Principles of categorization', in E. Rosch, and B. B. Lloyd (eds) *Cognition and Categorization*, Hillsdale, N.J.: Erlbaum.

ROSENBLATT, R. (1959) *Principles of Neurodynamics*, New York: Spartan Books.

ROTHWELL, R. (1975) 'Intracorporate enterpreneurs', *Management Decision*, 13, 3: 142–54.

ROTHWELL, R and ZEGVELD, W. (1982) *Innovation and the Small and Medium Sized Firms – Their Role in Employment and Economic Change*, London: Pinter.

ROTTER, J. B. (1966) 'Generalised expectancies for internal versus external control of reinforcement', *Psychological Monographs, Whole No.609*, 80, 1.

RUMELHARDT, D. E., HINTON, G. E. and WILLIAMS, R. J. (1986) 'Learning internal representations by error propagation', in D. E. Rumelhardt and J. L. McClelland (eds) *Parallel Distributed Processing: Explorations in the Microstructures of Cognition*, vol.1. Cambridge, Mass.: MIT Press.

RUMELHARDT, D. E. and McCLELLAND, D. L. (1986) 'On learning the past tenses of English verbs', in D. L. McClelland and D. E. Rumelhardt (eds) *Parallel Distributed Processing*, vol. 2, Cambridge, Mass.: MIT Press.

RUMELHARDT, D. E., McCLELLAND, D. L. and PDP RESEARCH GROUP (1968) *Parallel Distributed Processing*, vols 1 and 2, Cambridge, Mass.: MIT Press.

SAIC, (1988) *ANSim Users Manual*, Version 2.02, San Diego, California: Science Applications International Corporation.

SCASE R. and GOFFEE, R. (1980) *The Real World of the Small Business Owner*, London: Croom Helm.

SCASE R. and GOFFEE, R. (1982) *The Entrepreneurial Middle Class*, London: Croom Helm.

SCHERE, J. C. (1982) 'Tolerance of ambiguity as a discriminating variable between enterpreneurs and managers', *Academy of Management Proceedings*: 404–8.

SCHON, D. A. (1965) 'Champions for radical new inventions', *Harvard Business Review*, March/April: 77–86.

SCHULTZ, T. W. (1975) 'The value of the ability to deal with disequilibria', *Journal of Economic Literature*, 13: 827–47.

SCHULTZ, T. W. (1980) 'Investment in entrepreneurial ability', in *Scandinavian Journal of Economics*, 82: 437–48.

SCHUMPETER, J. A. (1934) *The Theory of Economic Development*, Cambridge, Mass.: Harvard University Press.

SCHUMPETER, J. A. (1961) *History of Economic Analysis*, ed. by E. B. Schumpeter, London: George Allen & Unwin.

SEXTON, D. L. (1987) 'Advancing small business research: utilizing research from other areas', *American Journal of Small Business*, 11, 3: 25–30.

SEXTON, D. L. and BOWMAN, N. B. (1984) 'Personality inventory for potential entrepreneurs: evaluation of a modified JPI/PRF-E test instrument', in J. A. Hornaday, F. Tarpley, J. A. Timmons, and K. H. Vesper (eds) *Frontiers of Entrepreneurship Research*, Wellesey, Mass.: Babson College, Center for Entrepreneurial Studies: 40–51.

SHAPERO, A. (1975) 'The displaced, uncomfortable entrepreneur', *Psychology Today*, November: 83–9, 133.

SHEA, P. M. and LIN, V. (1989) 'Detection of explosives in checked airline baggage using an artificial neural system', *International Journal of Neural Networks*, 1, 4: 249–53.

SHWEDER, R. A. (1975) 'How relevant is an individual difference theory of personality ratings?' *Journal of Personality and Social Psychology*, 43: 455–85.

SHWEDER, R. A. (1977) 'Likeness and likelihood in everyday thought: magical thinking in judgements about personality', *Current Anthropology*, 18: 637–58.

SHWEDER, R. A. and D'ANDRADE, R. G. (1979) 'Accurate reflections or systematic distortion? A reply to Block, Weiss and Thorne, *Journal of Personality and Social Psychology*, 37: 1075–84.

SLEVIN, D. P. and COVIN, J. G. (1988) 'Entrepreneurship and organicity: two key variables in small firm success' Paper presented at the *Eleventh National Small Firms Policy & Research Conference*, Nov., Cardiff.

SMITH, A. (1976) *The Wealth of Nations*, vol. I, book I, ch. VI: 42, Everyman's Library 412, London: Dent & Sons.

SMITH, N. R. (1967) *The Entrepreneur and His Firm: The Relationship Between Type of Man and Type of Company*, East Lansing, Michigan: Michigan State University Press.

STANWORTH, M. J. K. and CURRAN, J. (1973) *Management Motivation in the Smaller Business*, London: Gower.

STANWORTH, M. J. K. and CURRAN, J. (1976) 'Growth and the smaller firm – an alternative view', *Journal of Management Studies*, (May): 95–110.

STARK, W. (ed.) (1952) *Jeremy Bentham's Economic Writings*, London: Allen & Unwin.

STEVENSON, H. E. (1983) 'Entrepreneurship: hunting the heffalump', *Harvard Business School Bulletin*, (June): 50–1.

STEVENSON, H. H., ROBERTS, M. J. and GROUSBECK, H. I. (1985) *New Business Ventures and the Entrepreneur*, Homewood, Ill.: Irwin.

STEVENSON, H. H., ROBERTS, M. J. and GROUSBECK, H. I. (1989) *New Business Ventures and the Entrepreneur*, 3rd ed. Homewood, Ill.: Irwin.

STEVENSON, H. H. and SAHLMAN, W. A. (1989) 'The entrepreneurial process', in P. Burns and J. Dewhurst (eds) *Small Business and Entrepreneurship*, ch. 5: 94–157.

TIMMONS, J. A. (1989) *The Entrepreneurial Mind*, Andover, Mass.: Brick House Publishing.

TIMMONS, J. A., SMOLLEN, L. E. and DINGEE, A. L. M. (1977) *New Venture Creation*, 1st ed. Homewood, Ill.: Irwin.

TIMMONS, J. A., SMOLLEN, L. E. and DINGEE, A. L. M. (1985) *New Venture Creation*, 2nd ed., Homewood, Ill.: Irwin.

WASSERMAN, P. D. (1989) *Neural Computing*, New York: Van Nostrand Reinhold.

WIDROW, B. and HOFF, M. E. (1960) 'Adaptive switching circuits', 1960 IRE WESCON *Convention Record*, 4, New York: Institute of Radio Engineers: 96–104.

WILKEN, P. H. (1979) *Entrepreneurship: A Comparative and Historical Study*, Norwood, N.J.: Ablex Publishing.

WOO, C. Y., DUNKELBERG, W. C. and COOPER, A. C. (1988) 'Entrepreneurial typologies: definition and implications', in *Frontiers of Entrepreneurship Research*, Wellesey, Mass.: Babson College, Center for Entrepreneurial Studies: 165–76.

WORTMAN, M. S. (1986) 'A unified framework, research typologies, and research prospectuses for the interface between entrepreneurship and small business', *The Art and Science of Entrepreneurship*, Cambridge, Mass.: Ballinger, 273–331.

ZADEH, L. A., FU, K. S., TANAKA, K. and SHIMURA, M. (eds) (1975) *Fuzzy Sets and Their Application to Cognitive and Decision Processes*, New York: Academic Press.

Author Index

Aboud, J. 38, 159
Aldag, R.J. 57, 158
Aldrich, H. 69, 156
Aleksander, I. 82, 156
Anderson, J.A. 75, 156
Angleitner, A. 8, 156
Argyle, M. 30, 156
Atkinson, R.H. 38, 43, 156

Bechhofer, F. 5, 156
Begley, T.M. 37–9, 61, 156
Binks, M. 148, 156
Birch, D. 38, 43, 156
Bosley, J.J. 159
Boulton, W.R. 157
Bowman, N.B. 38, 162
Boyd, D.P. 37–8, 61, 156
Boyes-Bream, P. 161
Brockhaus, R.H. 29, 37–8, 40, 42, 156, 157
Buchholtz, A. 3, 6, 149, 158
Burns, B. 44, 157
Burns, T. 60, 157
Buss, D.M. 150, 157

Cantillon, R. 13, 157
Cantor, N. 7, 35, 52, 150, 157
Carland, J.A.C. 4–5, 157
Carland, J.W. 3–5, 42–3, 157, 159
Carsrud, A.L. 69, 157
Casson, M. 4, 24–5, 157
Chell, E. 3, 5, 9, 29, 55, 157
Churchill, N.C. 61–2, 149, 158
Clark, J.B. 21, 158
Cochran, T.C. 2, 158
Cooper, A.C. 58, 61, 70, 158, 163

Covin, J.G. 59–61, 68, 158, 162
Craik, K.H. 150, 157
Curran, J. 55, 163

D'Andrade, R.G. 33, 158, 162
Demtroder, A.I. 8, 156
Dickie-Clark, H.P. 55, 158
Dingee, A.L.M. 163
Dunkelberg, W.C. 58, 158, 163

Eddy, G.G. 157
Elliott, B. 5, 156
Endler, N. 30, 158

Filley, A.C. 57, 158
Flamholtz, F.G. 62, 158
Flanagan, J.C. 45, 158
Friesen, P.H. 43, 64–6, 160, 161
Fu, K.S. 163
Funder, D.C. 32, 34, 160
Furnham, A. 40, 148, 159

Gibb, A. 55, 159
Ginsberg, A. 3, 6, 149, 158
Goffee, R. 6, 55, 159, 162
Goldberg, L.A. 159
Gray, W.D. 161
Grousbeck, H.I. 163

Hampson, S.E. 10, 30–6, 52, 69, 149, 150, 159
Harwood, E. 2–3, 159
Haworth, J.M. 3, 5, 9, 29, 55, 149, 157, 159
Hebb, D.O. 79–80, 159
Hébert, R.F. 14, 22, 26–8, 159

Hettema, P.J. 44, 159
Hinton, G.E. 161
Hoff, M.L. 80, 163
Hornaday, J.A. 38, 159
Horwitz, P.S. 29, 157
Hoy, F. 3, 43, 157, 159
Hull, D.L. 3, 38, 42, 159

John, O.P. 159
Johnson, D.M. 161
Julian, J.N. 43, 159

Kazanjian, R.K. 62–63, 159
Kenrick, D.T. 32, 34, 44, 159, 160
Kets de Vries, M.F.R. 37, 55, 67,
   160
Kilby, P.M. 2, 42, 69, 160
Kippenberger, A. 44, 157
Kirzner, I.M. 24, 160
Kline, P. 32, 160
Knight, F.H. 20–1, 160
Koestler, A. 160

Lessem, R. 2, 160
Levenson, H. 39, 160
Levine, R. 55, 160
Levinson, D.J. 56, 160
Lewis, A. 148, 159
Lichtman, C.M. 159
Lin, V. 9, 162
Link, A.N. 14, 22, 26–8, 159
Lippmann, R.P. 82, 160
Little, B. 30, 156
Livesay, H.C. 2, 160

McClelland, D.C. 37–9, 42–4, 55,
   57, 149, 160, 161
McClelland, R.J. 9, 80, 161, 162
Magnusson, D. 30, 158, 160
Marshall, A. 17, 160
Meredith, G.G. 4, 37, 42, 45, 149,
   160
Mervis, C.B. 161
Mill, J.S. 16, 160
Miller, D. 43, 64–6, 160, 161
Mintzberg, H. 66, 161
Miron, D. 39, 161
Mischel, W. 7, 29, 30, 33, 35, 52,
   150, 157, 161
Mises, L. von, 19, 161

Morton, H. 82, 156

Neck, P.A. 160
Nelson, R.E. 160
Nord, W.R. 40, 157
Norris, K. 5, 161

Olm, K.W. 157

Palmer, M. 157
PDP Research Group, 162

Ricardo, D. 15, 161
Ricketts, M. 161
Ritchie, J. 55, 159
Roberts, M.J. 163
Rosch, E. 7, 35, 36, 52, 161
Rosenblatt, R. 80, 161
Rosenfeld E. 75, 156
Rothwell, R. 2, 161
Rotter, J.B. 39, 40, 161
Rumelhardt, D.E. 9, 80, 81, 161,
   162
Ryckman, R.M. 159

Sahlman, W.A. 36, 59, 163
SAIC, 136, 162
Scase, R. 6, 55, 159, 162
Schere, J.C. 37, 162
Schon, D.A. 2, 162
Schultz, T.W. 2, 25, 162
Schumpeter, J.A. 14, 22, 42, 162
Sexton, D.L. 38, 69, 147, 162
Shapero, A. 55, 56, 67, 162
Shea, P.M. 9, 162
Shimura, M. 163
Shweder, R.A. 33, 162
Slevin, D.P. 59–61, 68, 158, 162
Smith, A. 15, 162
Smith, N.R. 6, 56, 58, 70, 71, 163
Smollen, L.E. 163
Stalker, G.M. 60, 157
Stanworth, M.J.R. 55, 163
Stark, W. 15, 163
Stevenson, H.E. 3, 163
Stevenson, H.H. 36, 58, 59, 67, 163

Tanaka, K. 163
Timmons, J.A. 3, 4, 42, 46–51, 53,
   149, 163

Toulouse, J.-M. 64, 65, 161

Udell, G.G. 159

Vale, P. 148, 156

Wasserman, P.D. 82, 163
Widrow, B. 80, 163
Wilken, P.H. 38, 163

Williams, R.J. 161
Winter, D.G. 39, 160
Woo, C.Y. 57, 163
Wortman, M.S. 69, 163

Zadeh, L.A. 7, 163
Zegveld, W. 2, 161
Zimmer, C. 69, 156

Subject Index

achievement 91, 92, 95, 99, 102, 107, 108, 114, 118 motivation 37, 39, 43; motive 38, 39; orientation 45, 49

acquisition 66, 100, 101, 106, 111, 118, 122

Act Frequency Approach 150

administration 14, 20, 38, 57, 93, 96, 103, 109, 131, 145, 149

adventure 102, 103, 114

adventurous 71, 72, 145, 153, 154

agent of change 8, 24, 28, 154

algorithm 80, 83–5, 152

arbitrageur 24, 26

archetypes 8, 66

autonomy 3, 6, 7

back-propagation 81, 82, 136, 137, 152

Baudeau 13, 14

behavioural acts 7, 8, 33, 153

Behavioural Event Interview 45, 53

Bentham, Jeremy 15

biographical method 10, 82, 124, 147, 150

business: development 17, 61, 62, 70, 87, 92, 99, 107, 115, 136 plan 97, 103, 107, 130, 133

Cantillon, R. 13, 14, 21, 26

capitalist 12–18, 20, 23, 27, 28

case studies 11, 75, 86, 87, 121, 125

categorisation 6–8, 10, 11, 34, 35, 52, 69, 70, 73, 75, 82, 83, 87, 124, 125, 135, 136, 138, 143, 146, 147, 149, 150, 154

category: basic level, 70; membership 7, 9, 11, 35, 52, 125, 144, 150; semantic, 33, 35; subordinate level, 6, 150, 151; superordinate level, 150

change 8, 12, 14, 19–21, 24, 27, 28, 41, 68, 72, 73, 80, 82, 91, 94, 104, 109, 111, 119, 122, 124, 129–32, 134, 135, 136, 150, 151, 154

chaos 46, 99

Clark, John Bates 20, 21

classification (see also typology) 2, 3, 10, 20, 58, 80, 86

cognitive modelling 75, 83

commitment 45, 47, 59, 103, 106, 145

communication 66, 90, 114, 120, 133, 134

competencies 45, 53

competition 21, 132

competitive advantage 25, 28, 57

confidence 22, 28, 41, 43, 45, 48, 55, 71, 104, 121

configuration 65, 66, 152

consistency 30, 32, 34, 132, 149, 150, 153

contingency approach 55, 61, 64, 68

creative 6, 8, 94, 122; imagination 24, 28

creativity 7, 48, 49, 95, 128

Critical Incident Technique 10, 45

Darwin, C. 16

Davenport 21

decision making 23, 27, 64, 107

decision maker 13, 98

definition, problems of 1–7, 37, 44
delegation 62, 65, 74, 106, 120, 145
Delta Rule 80; Generalised, 81–4
demand 13–15, 19, 25, 119
deviant 37, 54–6, 67
displaced person 56
dream 95, 99, 103, 121

economic activity 1, 12;
    development 22, 38; event 148;
    function 12, 58; growth 27
economists 9, 10, 12–15, 18, 20, 28,
    147
economy 9, 12–16, 25–7
efficiency 19, 45, 90, 112, 131, 132,
    148
energy 16, 20, 47, 48, 73, 102, 103,
    111, 121, 122, 133
enterprise 6, 16, 17, 20, 26, 46, 49,
    109, 145, 151; culture 38, 131
enthusiasm 79, 90, 102, 103
entrepreneur (see also type of
    business owner): characteristics of,
    1, 4, 5, 7, 10, 28, 45, 46, 58, 145,
    149, 153; craftsman, 57, 58, 67;
    definitions of, 3–5, 26, 27, 45–9;
    function of, 12–15, 19, 26–8;
    opportunistic, 19, 57; psychology
    of,
    12, 147; role of, 13, 14, 20; types of,
    19, 20, 46, 56, 70
entrepreneurial: conglomerate 66;
    firm 54, 64, 66; flair 29, 89, 102;
    personality 1, 9, 11, 36, 44, 49, 52,
    53, 54, 69, 136, 147, 149, 151–4;
    spirit 62
entrepreneurship 2, 3, 7, 12, 22, 26,
    36, 42, 46, 54, 58, 62–65, 147;
    definition of, 1, 3, 24, 25, 46
equilibrium theory 27
error: function 83, 85;
    propagation 80; signal 83, 84
expansion 3, 62, 73, 89, 91, 111,
    114, 117, 118, 131, 132, 134
export 93, 94, 100, 108, 117

factors of production 14, 22
failure 4, 27, 38, 41, 42, 48, 91, 95,
    107, 143
family: 5, 11, 16, 86, 87, 92, 104,

110–13, 133; business 94, 129, 131,
    133; resemblance 35
financial ratios 151
firms: adaptive 66; bureaucratic, 61
    mechanistic 60, 61; organic 61, 64,
    65, 67; planning, 64, 65; simple 64
foresight 20, 22, 25, 28, 119, 145
formality 72, 92, 107, 120, 121, 123,
    124, 130, 151
founder 3, 5, 39, 40, 47, 87, 88, 93,
    100, 108, 115, 123, 129, 131, 144,
    145, 148
function: activation 77, 78, 81, 83–5,
    141; combining 77, 78; threshold 77
fuzzy boundary 73, 154

gamble 23, 28, 42, 96, 119
goal 5, 37, 47–9, 62, 64, 66, 73, 118,
    121, 122, 129
growth 5, 27, 47, 57, 58, 62, 63, 66,
    91, 101, 105–7, 109–11, 118
growth orientation 1, 10, 69–74, 82,
    86, 87, 121, 124–34, 136, 146, 151,
    152; declining 71, 73, 126, 127;
    expanding 71–3, 92, 99, 107, 115,
    121, 124, 126, 127, 133; plateauing
    71, 73, 87, 121, 126, 127, 133, 134;
    rejuvenating 71, 73, 126, 127

Hawley 21
Hebb, D.O. 79, 80
high profile 91, 98, 122, 135; image-
    maker 71, 72
historical perspective 9, 13
holistic 147, 149, 153
Human capital theory 25
human resource 90, 134, 145, 148

Ideal type 2
ideas-person 8, 71, 72, 154
image 71, 72, 91, 98, 108, 114, 122,
    125, 128
imagination 23–25, 28, 33, 102, 103,
    114, 119, 154
imaginative 8, 28, 43, 145, 150, 154
implicit theory 30, 86
independence 7, 31, 48, 55, 58, 106,
    109, 123
industrial sector 28, 41
infrastructure 62, 72, 131

initiative 3, 45, 47, 49, 65, 71, 106, 117, 130
innovation 7, 19, 23, 26, 27, 60, 64–6, 71, 129, 148, 152, 154
innovative 5, 6, 8, 13, 17, 18, 20, 23, 43, 57, 63, 65, 66, 71, 72, 104, 129, 131, 132, 147, 150, 153, 154
innovator 2, 5, 9, 13, 18, 19, 26, 28, 66, 122
interactionism 30, 52
internal locus of control 10, 37, 39, 40, 43, 47, 48, 56, 65
intrapreneur 2
invention 63, 135
inventor 19, 57, 70
investment 15, 17, 71, 91, 103, 104, 111, 130, 131, 135

James, W. 79
judgement 13, 17, 22, 24, 27, 31, 41, 47, 53, 132, 150
judgemental decision 24, 27, 41

Knight, F.H. 20–2, 26

latent variable 3
layer (see also neural network): hidden 79, 84, 136–42, 146, 152; input 79, 136, 137, 139, 141; output 79, 81, 82, 84, 136, 137, 139, 141, 142
leader 17, 26, 64, 65, 105
leadership 20, 23, 57, 58, 102
learning 4, 9, 38, 39, 48, 75, 77, 79–81, 83, 84, 96, 136, 137, 144; experience 4, 38, 96; law 79, 80; rate 84; rule 79, 80; supervised, 80, 81; unsupervised, 80
life: course 68, 73, 136, cycle 25, 56, 61, 82; style 38
locus of control 37, 39–42, 65; economic 40; external 39, 43; internal 10, 37, 39, 40, 43, 47, 48, 56, 65

management: style 55, 58–61, 67, 68, 120, 123, 128, 130; team 72, 74, 102, 106, 124, 128, 132, 133, 145, 151
Mangoldt 18

manufacturer 15, 16, 100, 102, 108, 112, 121, 130, 131
marginal person 54, 55
Marshall, A. 16–18
McBer & Co. 44, 53
Menger, C. 19
methodology 1, 10, 11, 30, 35, 68, 69, 74, 125, 144, 147
Mill, J.S. 16, 117, 134, 148
Mises, L. von 19, 23, 26
motivation 28, 37, 39, 43, 48, 95, 124, 129
motive 3, 15, 28, 38, 39, 118, 124

need for achievement 37–9, 65
need to achieve 10, 37, 38, 45
network 88, 92, 96–8, 103, 114, 118, 122–4, 143, 144, 146, 152
neural network 8, 9, 11, 69, 75, 77, 79–85, 125, 136–46, 152; architecture 82, 146; inputs 77, 85, 119, 152; momentum term 84, 136 *Net* 77, 81, 83, 85, 141, 142; neuron 77, 78; node 77, 79, 137, 140, 146; *Out* 81, 83, 85, 141, 142; output 77–84, 136–8, 141–3, 146; processing element 77–80, 83, 85; training 80–2, 84, 85, 136–8, 142–6, 152; weights 77, 78, 80–2, 84, 136–9
niche strategy 66, 106, 128

opportunistic 8, 19, 57, 67, 131, 145, 150, 153, 154
opportunity 4, 7, 12, 17, 19, 20, 24, 27, 28, 45–7, 49, 57–9, 66, 67, 71, 72, 88–93, 95–7, 99, 100, 104, 111, 118, 121, 122, 124, 129–32, 135, 145, 148, 152, 154; cost 13
organisational: configuration 65, 66; context 2, 64; structure 60, 61, 64–8, 132
owner-manager 4, 6–8, 42, 43, 45, 56–8, 62, 64, 65, 67, 68, 72, 82, 128, 148

parallel distributed processing 77
pattern recognition 8, 77, 146, 152
perception 24, 26, 27, 31, 32
performance 4, 8, 10, 37, 39, 41, 42, 44, 49, 60, 61, 66, 68, 94, 118, 136, 138, 146, 151

personality: assessment 70;
   characteristics 8, 10, 20, 53, 67, 75,
   87, 128, 153; construction of 10, 30,
   52, 69; constructivist theory of 10,
   34, 36, 52, 69; development 55,
   144; disposition 8; inventories 35,
   52; inventory 31; perceived 33, 34;
   rating 33; real 32; theorist 30–2;
   theory 29, 30, 49, 152, 153
   perspectives: (expert lay and self)
   29–36, 52; expert 45, 53; lay, 42,
   86; multiple 43, 53, 70, 149, 153
prediction 11, 83, 124, 136, 138,
   143, 147, 152
pride 102–4, 114
proactive 8, 22, 57, 65, 71, 72, 106,
   122, 131, 154
proactivity 45, 60, 145
product champion 2
productivity 16, 23, 148
professional management team 72,
   133, 145
professionalism 92, 120
profit 3, 5, 13, 15, 18, 20, 21, 23, 24,
   28, 42, 63, 95, 101, 106, 107, 118,
   148, 151; motive 3, 28; opportunity
   28
profitability 5, 6, 20, 63, 118
promoter 58, 59
prototype 9, 35, 63, 72
prototypical 10, 35, 70–3, 121, 124,
   125, 128, 130, 131, 134, 148, 149,
   154
prototypicality 11, 35, 36, 52, 69,
   82, 121, 125, 147
psychodynamic approach 67
psychological inventory 31
psychologist 10, 45, 52, 53
psychometric measurement 35, 53

quality 19, 23, 41, 45, 95, 105, 109,
   112, 119, 132

reactive 72
rejuvenation 73, 130
reluctance to change 72, 73, 129–31
reputation 49, 71, 89, 95, 114, 118,
   122, 124
resources 3–6, 23–7, 46, 47, 49, 58,
   59, 62, 67, 71, 72, 91, 96, 104, 130,
132, 145, 148, 154
restless 8, 91, 105, 150, 154
restlessness 71, 122, 131
retirement 132, 133
Ricardo, D. 15
risk 3, 13, 14, 18–23, 25–7, 37, 57,
   64, 91, 100, 104, 106, 114, 119;
   calculated, 42, 43, 46, 47;
   uninsurable, 18
risk-taker 9, 42, 43
risk-taking 3, 7, 28, 42–5, 47, 48, 60
role model 56, 102
root mean square (RMS) error 83,
   84, 86, 138, 146

Schultz, T.W. 2, 23–6
Schumpeter 5, 12, 14, 18, 19, 21–3,
   26, 42, 71, 148
self employment 38, 55
Shackle, G.L.S. 19, 23, 26
situational variables 44
skill 4, 16, 17, 20, 25, 46, 47, 89, 95,
   100, 102, 112, 123, 132, 134, 146,
   149, 151
Smith, A. 15, 16
social learning theory 39, 144
socialisation 38, 55, 63
sociological approach 67
sole trader 86, 92
stage of development of the
   business 1, 10, 11, 63, 69, 72, 82,
   87, 121, 123, 125–7, 136, 151, 153;
   established 70, 72, 73, 87, 95, 121,
   123, 126–8, 129, 130, 134, 136, 143,
   145, 151; post-start-up 70, 126,
   127, 145, 151; professionally-
   managed 63, 70, 72, 73, 87, 99, 107,
   115, 123, 126, 127, 130, 131, 133,
   134, 136
stages model 61, 62
start-up 55, 63, 70, 72, 73, 87, 92,
   136, 143, 151
static state theory 21
strategic behaviour 43, 66
strategic management practice 7
strategy 41, 43, 47, 64–6, 100, 106,
   121, 128, 132, 145, 154
success 4, 25, 36, 39–42, 45, 49, 62,
   71, 88, 90, 91, 94, 95, 98, 101, 105,
   107, 118, 132, 135, 151

successful entrepreneurs 4, 20, 29, 45, 53
succession 129, 130
survival 62, 96; of the fittest 16, 18

taxonomy 26, 66
technological innovation 19
technology 28, 63, 112, 115, 122–4, 128, 131, 135, 148
Thematic Apperception Test 38
theory of personality (see also personality) 10, 29, 30, 36, 39, 54, 144; social psychological, 29, 52, 54
threat 109, 131
Thunen 18, 26
tolerance of ambiguity 37, 47
tradition 15, 26, 28, 113, 129
training 25, 38, 39, 72, 90, 94, 120, 132
trait 10, 29–37, 40, 43–6, 49, 52–4, 68–70, 75, 149, 152–4; traditional approach 44, 49
transition 63, 73, 92, 123, 124, 133, 145
trustee 59
Turgot 14
turnover 87, 92, 94–6, 99, 101, 108, 110, 115, 118, 120
Type A behaviour 37
type of business owner 50, 51, 57, 70, 71, 82, 87, 92, 99, 107, 115, 125–7, 151; administrator 70, 72, 97, 126, 127, 130, 148, 154; caretaker 28, 70–3, 125–30, 144, 148; entrepreneur 70–2, 126–9, 133–5, 145, 146; quasi-entrepreneur 11, 70, 72, 92, 126, 127, 131, 154
typology (see also classification) 6, 36, 52, 54, 56, 57, 69–71, 82, 135, 148

uncertainty 13, 14, 19–24, 26–8, 47, 135
undertaker 15, 17

value 23–5, 49, 57, 83, 84, 87, 93, 95, 96, 104, 136, 152
vision 48, 66, 102, 103, 122, 145, 154

Walker, A. 20
Walker, F.A. 20
Wittgensteinian 35